IT'S JUST A BALL

Exploring The Complexity of a Simple Game

Jon Townsend

DARK
RIVER

Published in 2021 by Dark River, an imprint of Bennion Kearny
Limited.
Copyright © Dark River 2021

ISBN: 978-1-911121-93-0

Published by Dark River, Bennion Kearny Limited
6 Woodside
Churnet View Road
Oakamoor
ST10 3AE

www.BennionKearny.com

Cover image: Patrick Schneider; Unsplash

ACKNOWLEDGEMENTS

This book is dedicated to my children, who will one day have to find their own way through life. Remember this phrase: "The map is not the territory."

I would like to thank my wife, Sara – you've never given up on me. To my parents and sisters, your support over the years has only been outpaced by your love for me and my endeavors.

This book is also for all the coaches that helped me become the player, coach, and man I am today. Each and every one of you has taught me something profound. In your teachings, I have found a path in life that I am happy to pursue.

And finally, to you, the reader: this book may be about my story, but the game is yours. My hope is that you enjoy the book, but I want you to enjoy the game more. If you do nothing else, find a reason to smile with a ball at your foot.

TABLE OF CONTENTS

FOREWORD

It is a genuine pleasure for me to be asked to contribute a short passage towards this book. I was first introduced to Jon's work during my time running the 12-16's program at Wigan Athletic. The internet is awash with analysis, articles, and game reports but there are very few that consistently produce original quality, insight, and intellect. Jon's writing, on various subjects within the game, stood out to me and I became an avid reader of his work. Upon working with him, both remotely and in the Midwest of America, it was immediately evident that we share very similar beliefs in developing young footballers. As a coach, one's personality and past experiences shape the way you deliver, interact, influence, motivate, and engage young people to be the best version of themselves. The way in which a coach ignites young players is born from thousands of small experiences they have had in their life; the people they have met, the conversations they have had, the colleagues they worked with, the mistakes they have made, the evolution of training methods over time, the books they have read... Jon's journey as a player, coach and journalist means that he offers a great insight for young players.

There are specific teams and coaches throughout football history that heavily influence how coaching evolves throughout the world. To those who have studied the evolution of the game, most would include Guardiola's Barcelona, Catenaccio, Arrigo Sacchi's defensive structures, and Total Football; the latter has heavily influenced today's prominent style where teams look to control the opposition with the ball. The possession-dominant game that is now seen in nearly all of the world's most elite teams, should always be traced back to Cruyff's Dutch team of the 70's. Cruyff introduced tactical flexibility in terms of the system and formation, collective control with the ball, pinning the opposition in their own half, and counter-pressing when the ball is turned over. However, from a technical standpoint, the absolute requirement of Total Football was a high level of individual technique and this been a focus in Holland ever since. Jon's experiences in the Netherlands provide a foundation that will always be embedded in his core DNA. It has led to a demand for high-level technique through ball mastery and constant practice by encouraging creativity and freedom of expression. These core elements are key for all players, all ages, all levels.

Every player, regardless of age, brings their own unique skillset and profile. Whatever their identity is, and whatever strength(s) they have at a young age, is always the same strength they have a decade or so later. The job as a coach, therefore, is to make them more of what they are. Make them understand their identity and enhance what they have. Weaknesses very rarely become a 10 out of 10, thus making sure players understand what they bring – and then stimulating them to dedicate an incredible amount of time on that strength – that's coaching.

The best coaches will always use their experiences to make sure the player constantly searches for the next open door, becomes self-sufficient, and understands the dedication needed to hone their craft. Tactics play a huge part in football and coaches should know what the collective game looks like to then be able to unravel that to the specific age and ability level of the student. However, the X's and O's are not the true magic of coaching; this lies in individual development. Seeing that individual player grow, improve, and constantly search for that open door – that's what coaching is all about.

Tim Lees

PROLOGUE: AS THE BALL ROLLS

December 2014. At first, I could only think of the rushes of the cold wind coming off the Pacific as I walked on the sidewalk. My weathered cap soaked up moisture as I zipped up my raincoat and wiggled my numbing toes in my worn-out Reebok Classics. The thighs of my jeans were wet as a film of mist breached the fabric surface. I padded my pockets, hoping to find my wallet and phone. Of course, you left them in the hotel room, I muttered to myself. What was supposed to be a quick walk down to the lobby became a venture out into the night air.

A relentless wind tore across the San Francisco bay, ripping the colorful flags at Pier 39 against the poles that stood resolute against the harsh Pacific gusts. There was a cacophony of cable clangs and clashes; each gust was met with barge horns riding wild on the wind before colliding with the pier. Off in the distance, *out there*, a dense fog began its near-nightly ascent on the cityscape.

The chaotic noise brought with it a recommendation to return to the hotel room where my phone likely rang unanswered, buzzing its way across the desk and bumping into my laptop in sleep mode. Sleep mode. That's where I wanted to be, but a line of thought gripped me as I stared out across the bay – one that I could not shake. It was as though the sirens called me to edge closer to the water's edge at the wharf.

There I stood, unemployed for going on six months, and unglamorously having to shift career paths; any faith in myself was running on fumes (I was certain that any faith others had in me was gone). Part of me wanted to slip into the frigid inlet and meld with the darkness to glide away. The problem with hitting rock bottom, personally and professionally, is every idea seems like a solution to 'fix everything' and often arises out of thin air. The other problem is those ideas, upon reaching a comfortable cruising altitude, tend to have the engines cut out. Sure, you can glide for a while but, eventually, the descent back to rock bottom has a meteor-like intensity. Ideas and their accompanying confidence incinerate on the way down.

I thought about the witty quote often attributed to Mark Twain about San Francisco, "The coldest winter I ever spent was a summer in San Francisco."

As hyperbolic as the line is – there was no denying the cold of the night air, regardless of season, as it rips across the bay. Amid the December disorder assaulting the city and my psyche, I entered a small shop tucked in amongst countless others selling touristy treats and trinkets.

It was cold. I felt alone in a faceless city. I needed to figure things out.

Walking in and out of stores with zero intention of buying anything, I allowed myself to think those thoughts of a life lived differently – where I was not an abject failure, where I had a stable job and an intact career, where I had a sense of self-worth.

The exercise brought me to a clearing littered with homeless people sleeping in ramshackle arrangements on the sidewalks and in alleyways. Those that were awake weren't really *there*, so to speak. They, too, were probably at the mercy of their own sirens, perhaps allowing themselves to think the thoughts of a life lived differently, too.

As I stepped across a clearing back into the lights illuminating the imperfect San Francisco streets, the wind had more to offer. Rain. At first, it was annoying mist that dared to spit in regular intervals, but that soon turned to surges of rain sheets. A group huddled near a park bench hurriedly got up to search for refuge from the rain. I stopped, stood, and looked up at that foggy night, hoping to get lost in it.

I stood for an awkward stretch for a moment before resuming my walk to nowhere in particular. Then, I saw it. A cheaply-made soccer ball wandered and rolled unabatedly across the clearing, blown into my periphery and into my life by that damn wind. Perhaps it was some child's lost ball. Maybe it was meant to be discarded. My feet carried me after it, and I broke out into a stroppy jog, bounding gently on my heels with my arms outstretched stupidly downward as it rolled across the ground. I caught up with the lost ball and stopped it underfoot. I hadn't touched a ball in months. When I lost my job, my coaching job went along with it.

What's all this got to do with soccer?

Everything.

It has everything to do with that maddening game.

In that very moment – just like countless moments before – everything became simple again. The rust shook off my first touch. Juggles and keep-ups were the first actions against a deep depression and a harrowing rainstorm in the faint streetlights. Then came a real jog with that ball on my laces and underfoot. Shadows were outplayed as I threw feints. I pulled the ball this way and that, performed chops and cuts weaving through invisible opponents on the empty wet streets. The jog turned into a run as my rain-soaked jeans and black raincoat slicked through the night air with a sense of purpose. The jagged smile of the city's jaws opened before me as I ran through alleyways, on the deck boards of the pier, and up the steep streets back to my hotel.

Every few hundred yards, and touches on the ball later, nearby trashcans became goals. Vacant walls became reliable teammates who complemented me with a cushioned return pass. Curbs served as minor obstacles to scoop the ball over, or to pass against, to collect with my chest. Geographically, I was in the city by the bay; in my mind, I was back in the Netherlands playing *straatvoetbal* or maybe I was back in San Jose or Chicago playing pick-up games with my friends or on my own preparing for the next level – wherever that may be, back when things were simpler.

Approaching the hotel lobby, I began to wind down my excitement and assimilate back into my shell of self-deprecation and depression, but only for a moment because an idea gripped my spine and shook me out of six-month stupor. I walked the ball into the elevator as my clothes dripped across the lobby floor. I rolled the ball underfoot with each step, and the cloud-like cloak that hung over my head evaporated. This thing, this cheaply-made, scuffed up and discarded ball meant more to me than any other object that night. Once in my hotel room, I flicked my shoes off and kept juggling and doing moves against my shadow to make the moment last.

I then opened the laptop and vigorously jolted it out of sleep mode just as I had jolted my psyche back to life that San Francisco night.

And I began to write.

CHAPTER 1: FINDING PURPOSE

Some people believe football is a matter of life and death.
I am very disappointed with that attitude.
I can assure you it is much, much more important than that.

Bill Shankly

Each player's journey is unique. One of this book's driving forces is the exploration of the journey rather than merely focusing on the destination – the finished product, so to speak. Writing about my own experiences in the game, on a multitude of platforms, brought about another type of footballing journey. Through documenting the processes, exploring the emotive power of the world's game, and combining the theoretical with the actual, a collection of stories, insights, and studies for a global audience came to life.

The rationale for this book is multifaceted. Its delivery of the message is blunt and unapologetic. The topic for this book came about on a walk through San Francisco in December of 2014. Then, I wrote an article centered on the importance of players – especially young players – developing and fostering a relationship with not just the game, but more specifically with the ball. I knew from my own journey as a player and a coach that so much depends on that relationship. It's vital to experience the game beyond the drills and sessions. This is about how one can *feel* the game, and escape the world, if only for those precious moments when a player finds themselves with a ball at their feet.

Players develop in a variety of ways and environments, and this particular article recounted my own experiences growing up in the Bay Area of Northern California playing soccer, to my time spent abroad, most notably in the Netherlands. It was in the Netherlands where I, and my fellow players, would amass upwards of 10,000 quality touches on the ball every day through a variety of exercises, games and mini-games, and free play. This was central to our technical development and proficiency. It was also essential to making the game a lifestyle – to melding the activity with not only existing but truly living.

The Editor-in-Chief for *These Football Times*, Omar Saleem, a man whom I attribute and owe much of my exposure to, found the themes of the article quite interesting as well. His primary job is as a professional football coach, focusing on player development, and he has worked with the likes of Fulham, New York Red Bulls, Queens Park Rangers, and

Melbourne City F.C. It was Omar who also saw the potential of this idea as something different. He submitted the piece to *The Guardian*, which published it for a wider audience.

What hooked readers and practitioners was an idea firmly lodged in a simplicity that brought all opinions and criticisms to the table. The discussions and debates emerging from the article reached their own fever pitch. Some attested to the logic of the idea that players need thousands of realistic, repeatable, and game-centric repetitions each day – focused on the demands of an increasingly technical modern game. Others refused to subscribe to the idea – believing it to be too rigid and robotic to be taken seriously.

The world of player development is occupied by countless brilliant thinkers and legitimately-talented coaches – true teachers of the game. It is also cluttered with detractors who see the world through a singular lens. This book makes no promises about the most inexact science in world football – player development. It does, however, open the door to a world of stories, experiences, case studies and use cases, and theories on *how* and *why* developing that symbiotic relationship with something as simple as a ball can make all the difference to an individual's journey in the game – *but also in life*.

This narrative is only a snapshot analysis of a concept I fully believe in, regarding the development of technically proficient players. The goal of this book is to allow readers to view the game differently while not being tethered to any single methodical approach. Developmental concepts are generally met with resistance, and rightfully so. During the research and writing of this book, I constantly reminded myself that the sporting culture I grew up in is radically different in a multitude of ways. The types of resources, methodologies, exposure, the attitudes regarding training and competition – they have all evolved and improved.

On a personal level, growing up and learning to play in the late-1980s, establishing my foundational skill acquisition through the 1990s and into the early 2000s forced me to be creative in my individual development. There was no readily-available market for instructional resources other than hard-to-find books and VHS tapes. Social media, YouTube, and access to the Internet (and all its virtual communities) were still years away. Aside from the sporadic glimpses of international soccer on American television, true learning required the individual to create imaginative ways to put the work in.

The game is complicated, and this book is not an attempt to simplify it, but rather to explore the complexities to inspire others to enjoy the *feeling* of playing for the love of the game. Terry Michler, the winningest boys' high school coach in the United States, is a wonderful friend and coaching mentor to me. He has a fantastic phrase he tells players: "The little things make the biggest difference."

And it's those little things that shaped my development. Activities such as striking a ball against a wall for hours, dribbling up and down the streets of my neighborhood performing moves and feints I saw from a Coerver training video or flipbook in the twilight against my shadow, spending large chunks of my day in an empty parking lot playing pick-up games with people who didn't speak the same language I did (but spoke a common soccer language), training with my club team – these were activities, that in aggregate, helped develop a more complete player.

There is great value in doing the little things correctly. The idea that anyone goes from Point A to Z instantly is nonsense. Every great coach and student of the game understands and stresses the value of impeccable technique. Individuals must combine creativity and improvisation with structured training protocols and environments and instruction. Another lesson I feel must be learned is *persistence*. To be persistent enough to seek the game out and create opportunities, where few obvious options exist, is a life skill. Pick-up games, jumpers for goalposts, and street soccer bouts must become weekly 'filler' activities away from traditional organized team settings.

To better understand the importance of developing that relationship with a ball and in a larger context – the game – one must attempt to explore how various development systems function. Oftentimes, players emerge from a footballing ecosystem as products of a broken system; the ones that make it do so *in spite of* the system, not because of it.

Furthermore, many lack the technical refinement and body control necessary to compete at the highest levels for long stretches. These developmental elements stem from the cultural aspects of a particular environment. If that environment favors "bigger, faster, stronger," those are the skills and attributes that will be valued over "smaller, smarter, and more clever." This permeates throughout all levels of the game within an environment. Players are products of their environment. Those emerging from cultures and environments that celebrate and value technique optimize their abilities at the top levels. Those produced in environments focusing merely on physicality and athleticism are at a distinct disadvantage and must refine and hone their technical abilities when others are optimizing theirs. Players are conditioned to play a style centered on what they are exposed to, what gets them selected for teams throughout their journey, and what is valued at-large.

The mysteries pertaining to player development are intriguing. The exploration into the abstract and almost unseen methods based on persistence-training, deliberate practice, and systematic habit-formation (combined with the power of the creative mind) is often reserved for disciplines like music, writing, art, dance, and performing arts. The training approaches explored here unlock skillsets and intangibles which are merely the beginning. Many of these same methods help produce some of the world's best players.

Introducing...

At this point, I would like to introduce myself. Who am I, and how did I come to write this book? Let's talk about my qualifications. I want you to know who I am and, most importantly, who I am not.

As a player, I was talented, hard-working, and studious on the nuances of the game. From an early age, I wanted to learn about each position and deconstruct a skill to its procedural parts as a means of learning how to perform it myself. I became what is known as a 'jack of all trades, master of none,' which is not as boring as it sounds because this aspect of my path allowed me to see the game in various ways, and took me farther than I could have ever expected as a player.

By my mid-twenties, I realized the next step was to learn how to coach, which placed me on a path of studying different training systems, tactics, and development models not just in soccer, but in other sports, too. The goal was to learn about the inputs of player development methods to better understand the potential outputs of each method. This led me to write about the game from various levels, including tactical analysis, technical development methods, modeling, and deep-dives into figures and trends that have defined modern football.

Here is who I am not: I am not a former professional player. I am not a sports scientist, nor am I an athletic performance researcher. Although I hold a master's degree in the field of education and research analysis, and constantly conduct complex analysis in the corporate sphere, I am not a lab researcher. I want to make it clear that the case studies, analysis, and topics I discuss in this book are meant to intrigue and encourage exploration and critical thinking. The views that I present are my own, as are the stories that connect with the topics and methodologies in this book.

I am not a journalist, although I have done a fair amount of work in the field of journalism, including conducting high-level interviews, holding town hall discussions during the 2018 United States Soccer Federation presidential election, hosting and appearing on various well-known podcasts and radio shows globally, and being published as a long-form writer in well-known football publications on the Internet and in print.

Now that you know what I am, and what I am not, you may still wonder: in what ways am I just like you? What do I know personally about the game that you have struggled to understand or been reluctant or intrigued to explore in your own journey over the years?

My own path was normal for an American player who started out participating in a multitude of sports. I started playing soccer when I was four-years-old and soon found myself playing in the streets, parks, and on various club teams in San Jose, California, and around the Bay Area. I played in high school and in an academy-type environment in Bradenton, Florida, which no doubt helped me play in college. After a sub-par college experience, I continued playing, taking the nomadic post-grad route looking for games and competition. I wasn't a soccer prodigy, but I wasn't half bad either. I wanted to play on, as long as possible, as long as it was still fun.

The more I study the methodical training methods of elite players and talent pools, the more I find myself challenging this notion that the best players are born superhuman. In reality, the easy part is asserting that Lionel Messi or Zinedine Zidane are footballing geniuses, which they most definitely are. For me, the bigger challenge has always been about exploring how average becomes good and good becomes great through the measurement of Key Performance Indicators (KPIs) and analytics across a variety of methodologies and environments.

Soccer, like life, is about reflection. To descend down the rabbit hole of what makes a player exceptional requires an exhausting amount of oscillating analysis in a highly-subjective world that changes with the seasons. And so, this effort is about investigating soccer at the fundamental and possibly forgotten level. This is where most people's careers remain in the catacombs of *what might have been*, where the greats honed their skills long before they were the greats. That gritty, unforgiving form of the game played wherever the floodlights are off, the pitches are unkempt, and the crowds pass by without acknowledging the shadowy figures kicking a ball around. This may be the game's purest form.

There's a beauty of this version of the game, away from the big-money contracts, promising scholarship offers, and twisted reality shoehorned into notions of grandeur. This is real soccer – the people's game. It is dirty and rather unglamorous, and it has the capacity to take everything from an individual with no promises kept in return. Perhaps that is what draws us in – a sliver of the elite play under the floodlights at the end of the tunnel. But at the beginning of all footballing journeys is one constant – the ball.

CHAPTER 2: THE BALL THAT BECAME A COMPASS

When you get tired of walking around in San Francisco,
you can always lean against it.

Unknown

December 2014.

At first, I could only think of the rushes of the cold wind coming off the Pacific as I walked on the sidewalk. My weathered cap soaked up moisture as I zipped up my raincoat and wiggled my numbing toes in my worn-out Reebok Classics. The thighs of my jeans were wet as a film of mist breached the fabric surface. I padded my pockets, hoping to find my wallet and phone. Of course, you left them in the hotel room, I muttered to myself. What was supposed to be a quick walk down to the lobby became a venture out into the night air.

A relentless wind tore across the San Francisco bay, ripping the colorful flags at Pier 39 against the poles that stood resolute against the harsh Pacific gusts. There was a cacophony of cable clangs and clashes with each gust, met with barge horns riding wild on the wind before colliding with the pier. Off in the distance, *out there*, a dense fog began its near-nightly ascent on the cityscape.

The chaotic noise brought with it a recommendation to return to the hotel room where my phone likely rang unanswered, buzzing its way across the desk and bumping into my laptop in sleep mode. Sleep mode. That's where I wanted to be, but a line of thought gripped me as I stared out across the bay – one that I could not shake. It was as though the sirens called me to edge closer to the water's edge at the wharf.

There I stood, unemployed for going on six months, and unglamorously having to shift career paths; any faith in myself was running on fumes (I was certain that any faith others had in me was gone). Part of me wanted to slip into the frigid inlet and meld with the darkness to glide away. The problem with hitting rock bottom personally and professionally is every idea seems like a solution to 'fix everything' and often arises out of thin air. The other problem is those ideas, upon reaching a comfortable cruising altitude, tend to have the engines cut out. Sure, you can glide for a while but, eventually, the descent back to rock bottom has a meteor-like intensity. Ideas and their accompanying confidence incinerate on the way down.

I thought about the witty quote often attributed to Mark Twain about San Francisco, "The coldest winter I ever spent was a summer in San Francisco."

As hyperbolic as the line is – there was no denying the cold of the night air, regardless of season, as it rips across the bay. Amid the December disorder assaulting the city and my psyche, I entered a small shop tucked in amongst countless others selling touristy treats and trinkets.

It was cold. I felt alone in a faceless city. I needed to figure things out.

Walking in and out of stores with zero intention of buying anything, I allowed myself to think those thoughts of a life lived differently – where I was not an abject failure, where I had a stable job and an intact career, where I had a sense of self-worth.

The exercise brought me to a clearing littered with homeless people sleeping in ramshackle arrangements on the sidewalks and in alleyways. Those that were awake weren't really *there*, so to speak. They, too, were probably at the mercy of their own sirens, perhaps allowing themselves to think the thoughts of a life lived differently, too.

As I stepped across a clearing back into the lights illuminating the imperfect San Francisco streets, the wind had more to offer. Rain. At first, it was this annoying mist that dared to spit in regular intervals, but that soon turned to surges of rain sheets. A group huddled near a park bench hurriedly got up to search for refuge from the rain. I stopped, stood, and looked up at that foggy night, hoping to get lost in it.

I stood for an awkward stretch for a moment before resuming my walk to nowhere in particular. Then, I saw it. A cheaply-made soccer ball wandered and rolled unabatedly across the clearing, blown into my periphery and into my life by that damn wind. Perhaps it was some child's lost ball. Maybe it was meant to be discarded. My feet carried me after it, and I broke out into a stroppy jog, bounding gently on my heels with my arms outstretched stupidly downward as it rolled across the ground. I caught up with the lost ball and stopped it underfoot. I hadn't touched a ball in months. When I lost my job, my coaching job went along with it.

What's all this got to do with soccer?

Everything.

It has everything to do with that maddening game.

In that very moment – just like countless moments before – everything became simple again. The rust shook off my first touch. Juggles and keep-ups were the first actions against a deep depression and a harrowing rainstorm in the faint streetlights. Then came a real jog with that ball on my laces and underfoot. Shadows were outplayed as I threw feints. I pulled the ball this way and that, performed chops and cuts weaving through invisible opponents on the empty wet streets. The jog turned into a run as my rain-soaked jeans and black raincoat slicked through the night air with a sense of purpose. The jagged smile of the city's jaws opened before me as I ran through alleyways, on the deck boards of the pier, and up the steep streets back to my hotel.

Every few hundred yards, and touches on the ball later, nearby trashcans became goals. Vacant walls became reliable teammates who complemented me with a cushioned return pass. Curbs served as minor obstacles to scoop the ball over, or to pass against, to collect with my chest. Geographically, I was in the city by the bay; in my mind, I was back in the Netherlands playing *straatvoetbal* or maybe I was back in San Jose or Chicago playing pick-up games with my friends or on my own preparing for the next level – wherever that may be – back when things were simpler.

Approaching the hotel lobby, I began to wind down my excitement and assimilate back into my shell of self-deprecation and depression, but only for a moment because an idea gripped my spine and shook me out of my six-month stupor. I walked the ball into the elevator as my clothes dripped across the lobby floor. I half expected to feel the stinging stares of bewildered strangers, but this was San Francisco. Once in the elevator, I looked at a picture of the late comedian and actor, Robin Williams, with a quote that read, "I can walk down the streets of San Francisco, and here I am normal."

I found validation in those words, and I allowed a wry smile to escape. I rolled the ball underfoot with each step, and the cloud-like cloak that hung over my head evaporated. This thing, this cheaply-made, scuffed up, and discarded ball meant more to me than any other object that night. Once in my hotel room, I flicked my shoes off and kept juggling and doing moves against my shadow to make the moment last.

I then opened the laptop and vigorously jolted it out of sleep mode just as I had jolted my psyche back to life on that San Francisco night.

And I began to write.

CHAPTER 3: 10,000 TOUCHES A DAY

In the summer of 2001, I was fortunate enough to train in the Netherlands for several weeks playing with a local team from Enschede in friendlies and tournaments. At the time, I was 16-years old, and I witnessed the methods young Dutch players used to train, prepare, and learn the game. The approach they took was almost academic. The Dutch are truly students of the game. Soccer is the world's most popular sport, and that's also the case in the Netherlands, which in 2016 boasted over 1.2 million players active in club football – a figure that accounts for seven percent of the entire Dutch population.[1]

One morning, after playing a few hours of street soccer or *straatvoetbal*, I rode my bicycle near FC Twente's training ground, in Hengelo, hoping to see the first team train. What I found were teams of youth players, aged eight or nine, assembled on a small pitch not far from the main training ground corralled by a group of coaches. Each coach held a notebook and what appeared to be clicking hand counters. I stopped to readjust my backpack. I hopped off the bicycle and grabbed a bottle of water from a side pocket and dug out my scuffed-up football, and started rolling it underfoot as I rested and watched.

Each player had a ball and was assembled into groups of six. The youngsters dribbled freely in a small space, and touched the ball with each step, while the coaches spoke to one another and issued instructions to the groups. This was followed by a brief, coach-led demonstration of a sequence of simple ball movements and manipulations. Immediately, the trainer blew a whistle, and each group began a series of ball touches in near-perfect unison while the crew of coaches took notes and clicked away with the counters. It was evident these players were familiar with the movements and sequences, which were simple and game-realistic. They consisted of cuts, turns, chops, and drags at game speed. The duration of each set took only a minute or two as the players performed rehearsed ball movements in sets of 100-200 repetitions.

---

[1] CBS, Central Bureau voor de statistiek, retrieved from http://www.cbs.nl/nl-NL/menu/home/default.htm, accessed October 11, 2019; KNVB, Royal Dutch Soccer Association, 2016, retrieved from https://www.knvb.nl/over-ons/over-de-knvb, accessed 2019.

The volume of meaningful touches on the ball was important, as was the speed. But what really stood out was the variety of expression and creativity each player displayed at such a young age. These coaches and trainers were not producing robots. No single Cruyff turn or V-turn was the same for any two players. Each player operated in his own manner, and offered individual body literacy to perform the moves which – at a more psychological level – seemed to be an extension of their personalities.

After rounds of toe-touches, Cruyff turns, drag-backs, pirouettes, juggles, dribbles, or paired one-touch passing, the players rested, then rotated to a different station, and began another set targeting a different skill. Deep into each working set, especially with passing combinations, the players found a rhythm. Upon establishing that rhythm, their speed and smoothness of movement only improved and increased. The smooth movements on display were not learned that day, but were the result of countless hours and hundreds of thousands of meaningful touches performed by the players in their own time, at home or with their friends, *away* from the training ground. What I observed was a slice of Dutch soccer culture: a hyper-organized, regimented approach to tasks often in small spaces. This was how young players were taught to view technical training.

Before long, I was doing similar sequences – off to the side – because the fluidity of movement really surprised me, and I wanted to emulate what these young players were doing. I had unknowingly inched my way closer before one of the coaches noticed I was off to the side of the training area, playing on my own.

He jogged over and spoke to me in Dutch. Gathering my awkward stammering and shyness, the young coach deduced I did not speak Dutch, so in near-perfect English, he asked, "You want to play? You want to join today? We just started."

I was a bit embarrassed, but I agreed to join in, thinking I would watch with the coaches since I was older than the players.

An older, more experienced coach shook my hand and, placing a ball at my feet, said, "*Hup*, you start. *Stop*, you stop. Good?"

I nodded.

The instructions weren't complicated. There was nothing elaborate about the set-up. More movements were demoed by one of the coaches before the training session resumed. Each drill was a progression of the previous exercise, with each exercise and sequence adding on to what was previously performed.

Since I started after the group, I continued to train with a coach as the players moved to another field to play the older team – players closer to my age. After 60 minutes, I had simultaneously been exhausted and invigorated by this level of technical work and the attention to detail. As a relatively talented and competitive player, this exposed a glaring hole not only in my technical development, but that of most players my age back home.

At present, anyone can watch YouTube compilations of the world's top players and see a side of the game highlighting fancy individual moves. While there is nothing wrong with admiring and seeking to emulate those skills, the leap that needs to occur is the one away from the screen and to the training pitch, street, or court to practice those skills. I have always wondered how a young player sees value in structured repetition as a means to unlock the higher and more complex skills they see on the screen.

Terry Michler is one of the top youth coaches and (as previously mentioned) the winningest boys high school coach in the United States. Based in St. Louis, Missouri, a hotbed of soccer talent and culture in the U.S., Terry has dedicated much of his career to studying and applying Dutch training methods and models in his own coaching. What drives his curiosity, and investment of time and travel, in the methods used in the Netherlands, goes beyond a casual interest. Terry travels to the Netherlands each year and takes players from the U.S. with him to learn, train, compete, and live in a unique environment that is not available in the United States.

I asked Terry what some of the single biggest differences between how American kids view the ball, and their relationship with it, compare to what he has seen in Europe – most notably in Holland for the past 40 years.

"The biggest difference, as I see it, is the importance of the ball in relation to the game. We tend to isolate the two – the ball and the game; two separate things that do not relate or connect as strongly as they should.

"American kids like to 'show off' with the ball (juggle and tricks) just for the sake of entertainment. The Dutch kids value the importance of the ball as it relates to the game, and the outcome of the game.

"The Dutch kids are more 'protective' of the ball. The ball is the essence of the game – it determines everything that happens in the game. When in possession, creating opportunities to shoot and score; when not in possession, working hard and fast to win it back to try to score. I don't see that mentality in the American player – the ball becomes like the shoes – a talking point, not a fixture of importance to the overall game and the mentality involved with that."

Terry also hit on the cultural aspects that help highlight the differences between young players in each country.

"We use the term 'ball mastery' very loosely, yet the normal game in America resembles more of a ping-pong game – constantly back and forth, turnover after turnover.

"The soccer ball in the U.S. is an easy item to purchase with an abundance of colors and brands. Many clubs even have the players bring their own ball to training. My question would be, 'How much time do they spend with the ball away from training?' My guess would be not much!

"For the very poor in the world, a real soccer ball would be a luxury – a rolled up bunch of plastic or rags would suffice. With our affluence comes drawbacks – the hunger and passion lag behind; the desire for ball mastery is overridden by 'performance' tricks."

A Higher Standard of Development

Immediately after the session with the Dutch coaches, I conducted an inventory of my ability. The self-audit was revealing. My technique was not nearly as polished as I thought it was, and it was levels off players half my age. A trainer told me I had completed approximately 10,000 game-realistic touches throughout the workout. Then he hit me with a haymaker when he revealed that each of his young players was responsible for getting that many touches on the ball, every day, at least six days a week, and I should do the same. He informed me they would complete a variation of that workout daily, usually at home, and every player knew its necessity. He equated the touches with putting money in a piggybank – a fitting analogy.

My narrative aside, in the world of true player development, it is evident a visible gap exists between countries taking pride in developing talent, and those content just to qualify for a tournament or be on the same pitch with the world's best. The countries developing great players have figured out a culture-centered and formulaic way to produce the talent that fills their club football system at all levels of the pyramid. Obviously, the talent will be tiered, but *that is the point*.

There are more numbers at the base that perform at similar levels, which is why the foundation of the Dutch system accounts for the largest part of the system's structure. As talent levels increase, the numbers of capably-talented players decrease. By weaving culture and development, it is entirely possible to produce the bedrock that a national team program can build on – throughout all age ranges. The mysteries around building not only talented individuals, but a talented and capable *generation* of players, are what drives the game's development and coaching models.

Technically speaking, the approach for an effective player development system may very well be a combination of metrics, quality, and contextual elements. Increasing the number of functional reps each day, within the right competitive context, at the appropriate age ranges, builds a stronger foundation for a player to improve. The higher the level of play, competition, and coaching (quality), plus the higher the demands of each skill performed repeatedly over time (quantity), should produce a better end product.

In the Netherlands, as with other great footballing nations, scouts would have found these promising players through a comprehensive identification process utilizing the networking pathways that allow talent to advance from one level to the next. These scouts observe youth players in local competitions, and give players that perform and show promise the opportunity to join a professional-grade club for further observation and integration. The regional soccer development programs in existence in the Netherlands, whose aim is centered on the soccer education of these young players under optimal circumstances to become professional players, is critical to fostering a culture of technically excellent players who are capable of playing a distinctive brand of football. One must understand that the goal – at these levels and in these circumstances – is not to provide recreational environments for these players, but to discern each player's potential to become a professional.[2]

Iron Sharpens Iron

Talent development implies that players are provided with a suitable learning environment so that they have the opportunity to realize their potential.[3] Talent identification in the context of player development is no accident. The process is methodical and geared to assess those who are most likely to integrate well into a professional environment. In

---

[2] KNVB 2011b, Royal Dutch Soccer Association, retrieved from http://www.knvbrjo.nl, accessed September 2011.

[3] Williams, A. M., & Reilly, T. (2000). Talent identification and development in soccer. *Journal of Sports Sciences*, 18, 657-667.

notable footballing countries, programs facilitate soccer-specific development – at the requisite performance levels – that will emulate and hopefully produce professional-grade performance from a young age.

Another way to think of this process is in terms of iron sharpens iron, where the most talented, sharpest players make others of the same level better. The classification of players is essential within elite ecosystems to ensure performance levels don't drop to accommodate less talented players. The goal here is to establish a standard, and move upward from that baseline standard, not drop below it.

Another way to view this model would be through player tracking. A player at the top of a competitive playing pool might be categorized as A-Track, while players in the B, C, and D-Tracks also exist within the same proximal talent pool. An A-Track player requires other A-Track-level players to push his or her abilities. An A-Track player getting D-Track repetitions in a drill or a game, for example, can hinder development for the more skilled player.

Before delving into the theory behind the number made famous by Malcolm Gladwell's bestseller, *Outliers*, it's necessary to examine why there is a gap in youth development. Countries that plateau, stagnate, or regress in developing talent, generally lack one of the following: resources, culture, or leadership. The role of culture is arguably the most crucial aspect when developing generations of talented players. In order to develop world-class players, one must identify what "world-class talent" really is, before initiating quick fixes.

For example, the United States presents an ideal use case of having a surplus of resources but lacking the soccer-specific culture and leadership to achieve the type of progress that would churn out world-class talent. There's no shortage of rhetoric rife with claims that the United States Soccer Federation (USSF) follows similar methods that football's powerhouses follow. However, without the cohesive culture that aligns with the game from the grassroots to the professional level, the U.S. will continue to play catch-up to other countries.

Soccer's world powers produce players operating within a framework that aims to improve and optimize a distinctive style of play. For these countries, the sport at all levels is such a part of life that it is closely entwined with the larger political and social fabric of a culture. There, young players do not see soccer as a chore or extracurricular activity. Instead, they see it as a necessary part of their lives. The game is an extension of who they are, and what they want to become.

In countries struggling to produce world-class talent on a consistent basis, the gap has less to do with individual ambition, as every serious player wants to improve. The issue is lodged in the circumstantial and environmental factors that limit their progress and exposure. For countries lacking success on the world stage, the fracture lies between a country's culture and its soccer. To truly extract greatness, a stable developmental process must undergo a vetting process whereby it is practiced, fine-tuned, modified, challenged, and critiqued over time (and generations) until it is optimized.

In essence, the *how* of anything becomes easier to understand when you identify the *why*.

Ideally, high-level player development approaches and a culture that supports those methods have similar footballing values. They highlight the importance of players getting as much supplemental training as possible to become specialists and mavericks in their positions on the field. Such an approach requires an incredible amount of personal investment into devoting time and energy towards attaining meaningful repetitions with the ball outside of controlled and monitored playing environments.

10,000 Hours – Myth or Method?

According to Anders Ericsson, Ralf Krampe, and Clemens Tesch-Römer's famed case study – *The Role of Deliberate Practice in the Acquisition of Expert Performance* – it is not just the time spent practicing that is important; it is that the training must be directed at improving or developing a skill (deliberate practice).[4]

If one were to apply this theory to soccer, it would have to be in the context of honing skills in isolation, as real match play requires decision-making, creativity, improvisation, and situational factors that rote repetition cannot replicate. To this end, it is crucial for players with the potential to become a professional to receive or seek specialized training to develop themselves to the greatest extent. Learning in soccer involves acquiring new or modifying existing skills. Performing essential soccer skills is a requisite in being able to participate in the soccer game.

With any functioning system, there must be a process – a measurable input that yields a predictable output. Malcolm Gladwell's book *Outliers*

---

[4] Ericsson, K. A., Krampe, R. T., & Tesch-Römer, C. (1993). The Role of Deliberate Practice in the Acquisition of Expert Performance. *Psychological Review*, 100, 363-406.

suggests that, in addition to peripheral factors like luck and random chance, mastery of a specific skill takes no fewer than 10,000 hours of focused practice and performance. The research reinforces the validity of case studies lodged heavily in the theory that 10,000 hours dedicated to specific skills and tasks is one of many baseline requirements. But in soccer, 10,000 hours of application does not guarantee mastery; so how about 10,000 touches a day on the ball?

Admittedly, there are countless factors at play regarding whether a player becomes a professional. But what if the goal is to produce capable footballers at not only the professional level, but at all levels?

One example is the approach I experienced on the training ground in Hengelo. The Netherlands consistently produces technically proficient players. These players are products of a culture that values successful attention to detail concerning youth development, with scouting systems feeding the larger clubs. Ajax, PSV Eindhoven, Sparta Rotterdam, and Feyenoord soccer mills continually churn out talented players (output). The intrinsic dynamics of every player are unique and developed by many constraints, including maturation, training, learning, and environment, which all interact to form performance, and eventually reach professional soccer.[5]

Perhaps Rinus Michels' *Total Football* combined with the influence of Johan Cruyff and the *Clockwork Oranje* of the 1970s, along with the famed Coerver method, has paid dividends. In these systems, ball mastery is not only an expectation but a demand, as it allows players to dynamically affect a match from a young age, presumably producing happy players.

Don't Build a House Starting with the Roof

Optimal player development requires a sound foundation on which to build upon over time. Without developing the foundational skills and understanding the basics of technique, learning the more complex aspects of technical development are delayed and difficult to master.

The Coerver Method is one coaching platform steeped in both pyramidal and pedagogical practices developed by 'The Albert Einstein of Football', Wiel Coerver, and heavily influenced by Alfred Galustian.

---

[5] Davids, K., Button, C., & Bennet, S. (2010). *Dynamics of Skill Acquisition: A Constraints-Led Approach*. Champaign, Il: Human Kinetics.

The moniker is well-deserved as development under this system requires progression through a structured process, beginning with the basics of ball mastery, footwork, group tactics, passing and receiving, and eventually moving towards individual moves and clinical finishing.

The repetition leads to habitual patterns of play and techniques to a point where complexities become simple. Players integrating supplemental ball-centric methods can feasibly get 10,000 functional touches a day. And this method is no longer exclusive to the Dutch style (*totaalvoetbal*). Styles and tactics in other countries, at both the international and club level, all utilize tactics requiring technically sound players with the ability to interchange positions on the pitch; a skill acquired through relentless repetition.

Think about how the dynamic of possession has shifted to 'possession with penetration'. In other words, it is not enough to simply keep the ball. There must be a purpose with each possession and, to accomplish this, players must be confident on the ball to play out of the back and operate on both sides of the tactical game.

In South America, soccer has been a fundamental part of culture ever since its introduction to the continent. As a result, the blend of soccer with culture has resulted in periods of domination by South American players and nations. Three South American countries have won half of the 19 World Cup titles. South America has also produced, unarguably, two of the most influential and talented players of all time in Pelé and Diego Maradona (with regards to players who have won the World Cup).

However, in the modern era, the likes of Lionel Messi, Cristiano Ronaldo, and numerous others, have set a new standard of excellence in terms of footballing skill, creativity, and intelligence.

Worldwide, fans are captivated by the creativity, flow, flair, and 'completeness' of both the Brazilian *Seleção* and Argentina's *Albicelestes*. In these cultures and systems, players learn to maximize their effectiveness through rigid competition both at the club level and, territorially, in local games. The combination of futsal and street soccer stresses good technique and unrivaled creativity. Players are apt to get 10,000 touches a day.

Of course, these objective methods exist in the subjective world of soccer. One can look at the fact that the Netherlands has never won a World Cup, and other nations have shown they can beat Brazil and Argentina. One can also look at the Dutch influence on Spanish soccer's *tiki-taka* – stressing mastery levels of passing, receiving, dribbling, and finishing, and contend that Spain defeated the Netherlands in the 2010 World Cup Final using Dutch-inspired methods.

The Numbers Game

For all the dialogue about producing better players in the United States, England, or anywhere really, the approach needs systematic re-evaluation. Consider nations with a long history of producing generations of world-class players of a high playing pedigree. In these nations, professional clubs rely on dedicated assessments from scouts and coaches to identify players talented enough, and with enough potential, for a professional-grade developmental program. The business of scouting and its relationship to talent identification is 'coach-driven' and is mainly based on intuitive knowledge.[6] Producing the next Cristiano Ronaldo or Lionel Messi is unlikely, let alone producing a generation of them, but looking at the differences between players from countries hovering just above average at best, and encouraging players to strive for measurable development, is essential.

Proactive social experiments utilize metrics and data to reinforce theoretical claims. At the basic mathematical level, an average player can start working their way up to 10,000 touches and, ideally, amass between 60,000 and 70,000 *extra* touches a week. Over the course of a year, that number equals around 3.6 million *additional* touches on the ball.

Counting touches is merely a method of unlocking and revealing something much more important – a player's potential and confidence on the ball when executing skills and decisions. Measuring the potential of players within a talent pool is a method to indicate what player has a better chance of ultimately becoming an elite player.

Of course, this is all an inexact science. There are plenty of obstacles and other factors that affect players, such as the rate of physical and mental maturation, training frequency and quality, and a player's ability to learn and retain concepts and skills over time. All of these factors combine to yield diverse developmental patterns. Psychologically and physically, for example, differences in maturity can be extensive.

For example, there is a dominant opinion that players born early in the selection year often have the advantage of being bigger, stronger, and

---

[6] Meylan, C., Cronin, J., Oliver, J., & Hughes, M. (2010). Talent identification in soccer: The role of maturity status on physical, physiological and technical characteristics. *International Journal of Sports Science & Coaching*, 5(4), 571-592.

faster – and thus have a higher chance of being selected and advancing to the next level. The result is also what is known as "selection bias" as coaches, evaluators, and scouts opt to make choices primarily on physical factors, in addition to skill, intelligence, and technical performance capability, which may be secondary selection factors when they should be the primary ones.

Quality over Quantity

But what is the takeaway? Is this approach just another example of over-emphasizing the use of statistics and figures in the organic game of soccer? And even if a player doesn't reach 10,000 but only gets 1,000 touches a day on the ball, the figure is somewhat arbitrary. Ultimately, a country's soccer federation should identify what the ultimate end goal is, before drawing any conclusions. Is it winning a World Cup or many World Cups? Developing a strong domestic league that showcases and retains domestic talent? Very few players will reach the highest level, but the truly elite players tend to separate themselves from the talent pool. The goal might be to raise the bar for all players. The system is not perfect; players will still have a poor first touch, deliver an errant pass, and duff a shot, but players should see the benefit of spending more time each day with a ball.

Using the Netherlands as an example, based on the 2016 figure that places the participation level in organized club soccer at seven percent of the population, the odds that a player is successful rapidly decreases with advancement. Only 900 of more than 500,000 youth soccer players ultimately reach and subsequently play professional soccer. Only a fraction of that tiny percentage (.0018 percent) go on to play for the *Oranje*.[7]

A player does not need a coach to complete 10,000 touches a day, which is part of the larger problem. Young players assume they need constant guidance and supervision, and will not train (a cultural issue rampant with reward-seeking and needy players). Improvement occurs with correctly and consistently implemented fundamentals. The players at La Masia, Clairefontaine, La Fábrica, De Toekomst, Carrington, Melwood, and other academies understand the value of supplemental training, but most of those players accumulated thousands of extra touches *prior* to their acceptance in an academy. In fact, that may be why many of them

[7] Abbott, A., Button, C., Pepping, G. J., & Collins, D. (2005). Unnatural selection: talent identification and development in sport. *Nonlinear Dynamics, Psychology, and Life Sciences*, 9, 61-88.

were accepted in the first place. They separated themselves from the pack on their own. Coaches know those players put themselves ahead of the curve. And, unsurprisingly, when players get older, they are required to constantly increase their performance levels to maximize their progress towards becoming a professional player.[8]

It is easy to side with the quality over quantity argument, but the best players in the world did not take the chance – they played the numbers game. Perhaps 10,000 touches a day *is* like money in a piggy bank. The method is subjective, but there's truth to the saying, "The more you learn, the more you find you don't know."

---

[8] Elferink-Gemser, M. T., Visscher, C., Lemmink, K. A., & Mulder, T. W. (2007). Multidimensional performance characteristics and standard of performance in talented youth field hockey players: a longitudinal study. *Journal of Sports Sciences*, 15, 481-489 (adapted for overview of talented soccer players).

CHAPTER 4: WHAT'S IN A NUMBER?

I have not failed. I've just found 10,000 ways that won't work.

Thomas Edison

There's an odd allure with the number 10,000 in several aspects of modern life, away from the popularized theory[9] of the 10,000 hour rule. At its core, the theory is perhaps simpler once it has been deconstructed a bit.

Persistence is the key driver to attaining a goal, especially in the pursuit of mastery. An individual must dedicate an extraordinary amount of time towards an activity or pursuit, often in isolation, to achieve a level of perceived mastery. In other words, they must be persistent to the point others are not.

But what is it about the number 10,000 that intrigues people? It's a massive number, but still within the range of the attainable. Healthcare professionals and various medical associations recommend people walk 10,000 steps a day to maintain proper levels of activity and to promote good health habits. So, where did the 10,000-step recommendation originate? And more importantly, what happens to the body when it is forced to take 10,000 steps in a single day? The literal 10,000 steps-a-day topic was first popularized by the use of Japanese pedometers in the 1960s under the name "manpo-kei", which translates to "10,000 steps meter". In turn, a popular race distance for a weekend warrior is the 10K.

Returning to the research, and practical explorations regarding deep practice and mastery in sport, sports scientists and researchers tend to agree that physical, physiological, psychological, cognitive, and sociological factors are interconnected. Moreover, the amount of

---

[9] Ericsson, K.A., Krampe, R, & Tesch-Römer, C. (1993). The role of deliberate practice in the acquisition of expert performance. *Psychological Review*, 100, 363-406.

practice also plays an important role.[10] As obvious as this is, talent identification is centered on *current* performance in youth sports, which makes talent identification an inexact science. As a result, using workouts and exercises lodged in deep practice helps measure the sensory-motor domain in a young player, based on the assumption that the domain will continue to improve as the child ages and progresses in the sport while gaining experience, intelligence, creativity, and continuing to mature physically.

Pieces of the Puzzle

Getting game-realistic touches on a soccer ball with any sort of metric-based approach involves dedicating additional blocks of time and effort to a rigorous focus on technique, with a tiered approach to improving skills that are pieces of a much larger puzzle.

These skills start with learning a specific movement and then performing it unopposed in isolation. The next progression is performing it against opposition, and ultimately performing it in a game.

These components of skill, when trained appropriately, can allow an individual to gradually improve the speed, dexterity (use of both feet), smoothness, and overall effectiveness of performing each skill, because the action is trained in a repeatable manner that builds confidence levels and strengthens the mind-muscle connections necessary to perform a skill more and more effectively over time.

Generally speaking, the better players in a talent pool are those who do the simple things well, and with more consistency and more frequency than their teammates and competition. That is, these players perform each skill-based sequence with more efficiency, more often than their peers. For example, a player who has the ability to receive a pass with a clean first touch, with consistency, is likely a more dependable player in other skillsets such as shooting and dribbling. Although this may be simple, it is not as easy as it looks on paper.

Johan Cruyff once said, "Playing football is very simple, but playing simple football is the hardest thing there is." Cruyff's quotes and his influence on the game remain timeless, but this one offers a unique perspective into the difficulty of doing the little things well and with consistency. When others fade or lose focus, the high performers stand

---

[10] Fernández-Rio, J. & Méndez-Giménez, A. (2014). Talent detection and development in soccer: a review. *Journal of Sport and Health Research*, 6(1):7-18.

out because they have trained at a level that others have not. Additionally, they can exploit the lapses and mistakes of those who have not matched their preparation level.

Of course, other reinforced factors play a role, too, such as position, game intelligence, and composure – all of which are directly honed through repetition, game-realistic training scenarios, and acquiring experience in competitive environments and games amassed over several years. Those players who have not dedicated additional time to executing game-specific skills are likely to be less reliable during periods of actual performance (match play). The acid test for learning skills and training towards a purpose is during competitive play because it is the *performance* that gets assessed since it is on display.

Addressing the Assumptions

At its highest levels, professional soccer is unique because of its popularity, and the beauty of the sport is that there is no right or wrong way to play it.

Soccer is also a game that is heavily influenced by specific inputs that are always evolving, such as culture and environment. The sport operates in a truly global talent pool. In spite of the high rate of failure that surrounds the journey, many young players all over the world leave their homes to pursue a professional career in soccer.[11] To this end, the 10,000 touches a day theory has a few basic assumptions that should be addressed to clear up any misconceptions.

First is the focus placed on 'counting' that underpins the methodology. The training method is not simply about counting, and the objective is not to merely count touches like some sort of soccer-playing calculator. Additionally, the differences between a theory of spending 10,000 hours playing soccer and getting 10,000 touches a day on the ball are not the same.

Although these approaches and systems have similarities, the latter is but one of many components involved in skill mastery. There are many factors and circumstances that must align for a player to reach the highest levels in the game, all of which can be unpredictable. There is no instruction manual for producing elite players. In short, getting 10,000 touches a day on the ball in a functional way that transfers to higher levels of game performance is one piece of a smaller puzzle

---

[11] Bourke, A. (2003). The dream of being a professional soccer player. *Journal of Sport & Social Issues,* 27(4), 399-419.

compared to the much larger puzzle of achieving overall mastery in performing specific skills.

I once gave a talk where I was challenged on the topic. Someone in the audience of coaches asked if they commuted to work every weekday for seven to ten years to amass 10,000 hours, would they be an expert driver. Initially, I tried not to laugh or be rude as I knew where they were going with this question and its logic.

I stated that an individual can sit in traffic for 10,000 hours, but that does not make that person an expert at driving, nor would it make them a professional behind the wheel. It would make them proficient in that routine and familiar with its nuances and idiosyncrasies. I said they are experts at sitting in traffic. The audience chuckled. I added that what they *are* experts in would be in the basics of driving and making decisions on the road for that commute, but they are not likely to be training towards something specific like cornering or using race techniques and tactics. To reinforce my point, the driver would be going through the motions specific to that commute, but they would not be training the same skillsets that a Formula 1 driver would be focusing on each session.

The major takeaway, here, is the understanding that 10,000 hours or touches are grounded in skill-based activities. Doing 10,000 repetitions of anything can be detrimental if that specific activity is not approached and executed correctly. Habits form with repetition, regardless of whether those habits are good or bad. Understanding the actual processes of true elite development is essential for arriving at sound conclusions derived from practice. Simply labeling something "elite" does not make it so.

The second assumption questions whether players, especially late-bloomers, actually have the 10,000 hours to develop into great players available to them. That is, if a player is 15-years-old and decides he or she wants to dedicate their efforts to becoming a professional player, is it too late? Moreover, is getting 10,000 touches a day going to make their dream a reality? In short, by the time a player is 15-years-old, their path is largely already determined (although, of course, there are exceptions) – not by them, but by the game itself. As harsh as this sounds, in a truly global talent pool, the game waits for no player to catch-up to the ever-increasing performance levels in top talent pools. Should a player decide to "get serious" entering adolescence, they can certainly find success in the game.

However, the window for becoming a truly elite player (one that may play the game professionally) is drastically reduced because, in a global talent pool, others always stay the course and set the pace when others taper off.

Furthermore, the plethora of externalities and contributing elements that must fall into place for a player to "make it" suggest that merely spending time playing the game isn't the answer.

So, we can generate an equation; a simple one:

$$Time\ spent\ playing + Quality\ of\ the\ environment = Opportunity.$$

Additionally, "making it" is a subjective term. Being able to start on a youth team, playing for a high-level and competitive club team, and earning a scholarship to a university would be considered "making it" in the United States but, elsewhere, that might be failure.

Research indicates that there is not a single type of factor that leads to success, nor is there a model that could relate to all countries or be applied to all sports.[12] However, a player who devotes time towards getting 10,000 game-realistic touches a day on the ball in areas that makes them higher performers, over the course of their development, is expediting the process in which they're becoming not only technically proficient, but technically superior to others in the same talent pool.

A player with the bandwidth to train and play *more often* builds a deeper connection with the contextual and experiential elements of the game and is able to develop the mentality and physical literacy to outplay and outperform others. If we layer training, access to the game, competition, and coaching, into the mix as well, that can be of further benefit.

That individual is playing a numbers game and is probably getting close to ten times the number of functional, supplemental repetitions with the ball compared to other players within similar talent pools. In other words, the skills or scenarios are fewer for a player taking a more conventional development route compared to a player on the more involved journey loaded with deep practice elements. That player on the more focused track has experienced a higher frequency of play, and has

---

[12] De Bosscher, V., De Knop, P., Van Bottenburg, M., & Shibli, S. (2006). A conceptual framework for analysing sports policy factors leading to international sporting success. *European Sport Management Quarterly*, 6(2), 185-215.

practiced those same skills and scenarios countless times more and at a higher level.

Top youth clubs and programs in world soccer seek the top players well before any mention of "elite" can be determined. Evaluating the top percentage of players deemed "the best" in a given talent pool is paramount. As a result, there is a pressing need to identify and nurture talents with the realistic chance of being elite players. This means they are already well ahead of their age group in terms of ability and learning capacity as it relates to the sport.

Research also indicates that there are five stages for talent identification and nurturing: detection, identification, development, confirmation, and selection.[13]

The third assumption is that a developing player must immediately compete with the best players in their age group in the world. Although this is partly true, it's also misguided. In reality, most players must first be better than the other players in their competitive and respective talent pools. A player dedicating additional time to a specific skill – such as dribbling or working on passing and receiving the ball proficiently – in comparison to members within the same talent pool who spend little-to-no additional time developing these same skills, is structuring their developmental path – diverting it away from that of the status quo.

That being said, the leap from above-average to elite is massive, and young players need high levels of success – pushing their abilities, reinforcing their actions, and being challenged enough – to stay confident and competitive. This means players should skip a level or two to push themselves and test their ability, but they still have to climb the ladder. Skipping too many rungs is not the answer.

In essence, the individual seeking out more playing opportunities and performing additional repetitions is knowingly or unknowingly setting the pace for others to keep up or be left behind. Intentional immersion in sport-specific activities leads to habit-formation. We must keep in mind that, at early ages, research has shown that there is a massive benefit to children playing multiple sports and developing high levels of physical literacy and interpersonal skills. The balance between focusing on one sport and spreading effort and energy too thin is tricky.

---

[13] Vaeyens, R., Lenoir, M., Williams, A.M., & Philippaerts, R.M. (2008). Talent identification and development programmes in sport. Current models and future directions. *Sports Medicine*, 38(9), 703-714.

The accumulation of repetitions – in addition to duration, quality, and intensity (blocks of time set aside for additional and specific task training) – plays a major role in how well an individual improves in direct comparison with those who choose not to dedicate time to the same tasks.

The fourth assumption is that getting 10,000 touches a day produces robotic players. Returning to another timeless Cruyff quote, "Technique is not being able to juggle a ball 1,000 times. Anyone can do that by practicing. Then you can work in the circus. Technique is passing the ball with one touch, with the right speed, at the right foot of your teammate."

On the surface, many believe Cruyff was devaluing repetition. However, what he was addressing is application of the skill. It may take an individual any number of times to perform a skill well, but none of that matters in the context of a game if they cannot apply it at the appropriate time. When performed correctly and functionally – that is, with match-realistic applications – the only mechanical part about this training method is its systematic breakdown: the framework and tallying of metrics. Robots follow commands and processes, and don't think freely. Training within a framework that allows players to expedite their technical skill while experiencing more actions in meaningful competition does not create robots; it creates free-thinking specialists on the field.

Discover the Plasticity of the Practice

An inevitability to the process is that a player attempting to crank out thousands of touches on the ball without thought, or a clear training objective, will rush through the exercises. As a result, the process fractures and fragments the functionality of the exercise, and compromises the quality of each movement. Any task-specific training requires a delicate balance between machine-like persistence and human creativity. A player jogging 10,000 meters with a soccer ball at his foot through the streets is creatively getting match-realistic touches on the ball, fitness work, and will need to execute a variety of skills that could be used in real competition (changing direction with the ball, stopping the ball, acceleration, etc.).

The systematic approach to 10,000 touches a day does not allow a player to do the difficult tasks without mastering the simple ones first. Obviously, players who are taught by stale, robotic coaches (or stale, robotic methods) are likely to become robotic players on the field. How a player trains is how they play in matches. Such rigid tendencies are easy to see in over-structured (often scripted) sports like American Football, where plays are pulled from a team's playbook, and coaches orchestrate and coordinate any and all movements and plays on the gridiron.

Soccer is organic, though. A player starting out with 10,000 touches a day must start in the rigidity of the workout – counting repetitions in structured exercises such as various turns, juggles, dribble patterns, and passes with a partner or against a wall. The crux of the methodology is not to start off at 10,000 touches a day, but rather to devote *time* to their game to the point they develop a connection and relationship with the ball.

Those who respect the process without coveting an undefined end-state or result set themselves up for more success than those who do not allow the process to work. While it is important to imagine a desired end-state and set an attainable target, obsessing over something that requires concentration on the process can lead to frustration and burnout.

Ironically, in the research for this book, I found people certainly put forth quite the effort to be more robotic in their daily activities, often unconsciously. People are creatures of habit. We live in a world where everything is counted, charted, cataloged, analyzed, and reviewed. Metrics and analytics dictate decisions. People wear global positioning system-enabled (GPS) watches when they run, to record and track the distance they cover. Smartphone applications count caloric intake and automate any number of tasks for the user. Society, in an ever-changing digital age, values metrics and assigning numerical valuations to everyday tasks.

These days, people are conditioned to track progress through the use of metrics as a validation step. Some people are driven by the idea of reaching a measurable reward at the end of the road for many of the tasks they undertake. Jobs, educations, and social interactions revolve around quantitative and qualitative goal-setting and goal-attainment. People are driven by Key Performance Indicators (KPIs) and metrics to such a degree that they determine and define lifestyles and livelihoods!

Raw metrics, however, provide only a partial glimpse of the process involved in measuring talent, especially in young players. Context and environment are factors that are important considerations. Additionally, the way that people learn, and the manner in which they retain information, is crucial. There has been a shift from the unitary perspective to the multi-dimensional model of talent. According to Deborah Eyre's book *Able Children in Ordinary Schools*, the traditional view of talent has been linked to the idea of ability or intelligence as genetically inherited and measurable through specific tests.[14] The context of intelligence is less academic and more related to application. A soccer player who can create, solve problems, and think their way through a problem on the field demonstrates Eyre's point. For players to truly excel, they must exhibit the ability to perform tasks *intelligently*.

The Role of a Cultivating Culture

Another contributing factor regarding talent acquisition and progression is the culture a child grows up in. Regardless of how revolutionary the training methods are for a player, without a true footballing culture, the player's opportunities begin to wane. For example, the culture of a country tends to be reflected in the type of footballers they produce. The frequency, quality, and level of immersion of soccer in the United States differ from how the game is played and learned elsewhere, especially in countries with cultures directly affected by (and revolving around) the world's game.

Growing up, I experienced the melding of the theoretical with the actual. Perception is the catalyst for improvement. I played nearly every day. My friends and I played for hours after school and over the weekends. We *made time* to train even though I never really considered it "training." I just saw it as playing. This awareness reinforced the notion that sport can be an extension of life. That being said, my experience and upbringing is not the typical American soccer player's journey. I grew up in an area with a rich soccer culture. Many of my friends were from immigrant families where soccer was the dominant sport.

The Dutch, for example, are known for celebrating structure and efficiency of space in a country where land is incredibly limited and subject to floods. Levies and floodplain pumps help preserve land and prevent flooding. As such, playing space is limited, so players take to the courts and streets to play *straatvoetbal* and team-sessions are often on shared pitches. Being creative and organized in life is important, and similar qualities produce technically-proficient, creative players who are used to playing in confined spaces and entering a cohesive football system to identify talent.

I asked Terry Michler, one of my coaching mentors and Dutch soccer expert, about how the Dutch view space and how it affects their training approaches and gameplay.

---

[14] Eyre, D. (1997). *Able Children in Ordinary Schools*. London: David Fulton Publishers.

"The Dutch people, by their very nature, are very attentive to detail; structured, organized, and frugal. When you consider the smallness of their country, and the fact that water covered much of it, it is amazing what they have done to create the landscape that they have. They are the best space engineers and managers in the world. With such limited space, they have managed to not only build on it, but have built some of the most modern versions of building and bridges anywhere. Space is the operative word to the Dutch. Whether it's soccer or life, space dominates their thinking and way of going about their business. In soccer, the major theme is to find and exploit space."

I noticed the value of space economy when I first traveled to the Netherlands and could see what Terry meant. He continued, "This is done with the combination of intelligence, attacking and possession – intelligence through vision and awareness, attacking in going to goal and scoring, and possession in that having the ball allows you the opportunity to advance the ball and score goals. The importance of having the ball places a very high value on the relationship each player has with the ball. It is the ball that determines everything that happens in the game; thus, develop a relationship with the ball that will allow you to use it in the most efficient and effective way."

Evaluating the concept of training perception in soccer-crazed countries, against countries where football is less popular, is essential in understanding the type of player each environment is likely to produce.

A main difference is the way dedicated players view training. The dedicated players always seem to stay after training and work on their individual games. Those who leave generally go home and still train, logging additional hours on the areas of their game that require the most extra work. In essence, training is rarely 'over' as players push to stay on the professional track.

Compare such a mindset to a sporting culture that doesn't stress the 'game away from the game,' and it becomes clear what is missing. A player's perception of training as a function, and the culture a player exists in, are inextricably linked. In a setting with players who view training as 'a chore' and who, as a result, cannot wait for training sessions to end, the level of play tends to stagnate. It's the same in environments that view training through a less-positive lens… where youth players tend to see the game as an extracurricular activity instead of as a lifestyle.

Contrary to what many believe, talent alone plays a limited role in the development of elite athletes. Accumulated practice and associated factors (such as coaches or facilities) are more relevant – necessary even – to becoming an expert in a sport, and being able to perform with success at a high level.[15] Additionally, factors such as maturation and the nurturing effects of parents, coaches, and the specific environment itself, allow talent to sift itself from the pack, as do factors such as resilience and adversity. Those who are willing to devote more time to their craft are likely to be those who view obstacles as molehills and not mountains.

Naturally, in non-soccer cultures, the idea of getting 10,000 touches on the ball in a month or two, let alone in a day, is considered excessive. At most, players touch the ball 200 times in an average training session and only 30-40 times in match play, and therein lies part of the problem. Players do not spend nearly enough time on the ball! The supposition that conventional (not supplemental) training provides a player with a sufficient number of touches on the ball has influenced the collective American soccer circle.

Taking Technique to Task

Tasking a player to dedicate significant blocks of time on ball work is no small feat. When performed at the right intensity, for extended periods of time, technical workouts (like fitness-based work) place an individual under duress almost immediately. Tactics aside, technical work is often underserved during group training sessions, yet is often the difference between dominating the ball and being dominated during match play. Isolating the components of the game down to specific requirements, per position, is paramount to the success of any player searching for ways to improve their technique.

A center midfielder should constantly work on how best to receive the ball in a 360-degree spatial capacity hundreds, if not thousands, of times a week to ensure the feat is automatic during meaningful competition. A target forward must train with a focus on receiving a ball out of the air with their chest, feet, or thigh and protecting it from the opposition before turning and hitting the target consistently. These tasks require repetition in a variety of ways, such as unopposed or opposed scenarios, to build and strengthen skills.

Such endeavors require a fair degree of rehearsed repetition – often at frequencies far exceeding what a typical technical session allows. In fact,

---

[15] Helsen, W.F., Hodges, N.J., Van Winckel, J., & Starkes, J.L. (2000). The roles of talent, physical precocity and practice in the development of soccer expertise. *Journal of Sports Sciences,* 18, 727-736.

deep practice and elevating the training level may go against the grain of what the culture expects and values at a specific age. Ironically, in American sports, such repetition-heavy tactics are used to great effect in sports like basketball (jump shot practice, free throw training), and baseball (batting practice, fielding infield balls).

When I first traveled to the Netherlands, I took part in training sessions with two teams. One was comprised of Dutch players, and the other was made up of American players from Texas on a six-week training trip. The team from Texas was assembled as part of a selection process, with each player representing some of the strongest youth club teams in the state. Since I was a late addition to the team, and not from Texas, I was added to their roster as an alternate player, which meant any playing time would be scarce. As a result, I opted to find a local youth team to play for, to maximize my chances of learning something and improving.

The Dutch team was a local club in Enschede that took me on as a courtesy to my host family. Their son was the team's playmaking center midfielder. I trained with both teams, sometimes twice a day. The differences between the teams were staggering. The American team was athletic and fast, but it lacked technique and tactical discipline. Every training session and game was played at breakneck speeds, and the players took every opportunity to let their egos run the show.

We often played on large fields and ended with stagnant shooting lines where players seemed to test how hard they could blast the ball over the goal. The Dutch team played a more rhythmic style that was based on possession and quick transitional play. The training sessions were structured around drills that stressed technique, ball movement, positional interchange, and each drill would scaffold to a larger, more game-realistic concept. The size of the playing area was significantly smaller and was often split into grids or "zones" designed to teach tactical discipline, and space economy, on top of the technical work.

I quickly realized I would not succeed with the Dutch team where players were selected based on ability over physical attributes – unless I worked on my technical game and tactical understanding. The two elements are connected as the better the technical level, the quicker one can play within a tactical system. My technique lacked the polish of my teammates. The ability and intelligence required to play at a more intelligent and faster speed of play required technical skills that needed to be expediently instilled into my game.

After the first training sessions with the Dutch team, the coach approached me and asked me, "Do you play football at home away from the training?" I looked at him and nodded.

He studied me for a brief moment and said, "Not enough. You need more practice on the ball. You are now in a team that needs you to be a master on the ball. And you need to be smart with it. Smooth and reliable, you understand?"

Again, I nodded.

He then said, "You must go everywhere with your football. Spend hours on it. Teams in the USA do not do this for you, but to play with this team, you must be better on the ball. We cannot play our system with players who cannot do what we ask with the football."

Again, I nodded... as he rolled a ball to me and ushered me along, back into the training mix.

CHAPTER 5: WHAT GETS MEASURED GETS MANAGED

One question I regularly receive is, "What does training to get 10,000 touches a day look like?" This is a good place to start and, naturally, the answer will vary from one environment and skill level to the next.

The first point to make here is about the number itself. Whether a player gets 1,000 excellent, game-realistic movements or 10,000 pointless touches is an important consideration. Quality must take precedence over quantity, but there are ways to combine the best of both worlds.

In turn, there are universal elements that add structure to this training method, such as "chunking" or segmenting movements together, and "sequencing" or the combination of one movement to another. The training itself may be daunting at first – especially to those viewing it strictly in terms of rigidly setting up cones and grids, and monotonously performing simple movements until fatigue and boredom set in. I have seen this firsthand as a coach.

The next point is crucial. For most players, training is more than seeing cones set out, wearing fancy training gear, and seeking the approving eyes of a coach.

To them, it is far simpler. It involves a player and a ball.

Over the years, I have presented this method to clubs and coaches looking to change the way their teams dominate the ball. I would explain every term on paper or through a presentation, but the real details are best demonstrated on the pitch.

There, it is easier to see how the segmentation of skills, performed for a number of repetitions, forms a set. As training progresses, new skills come into play, and new factors layer on to enhance movement and reinforce the details. Then, the volume can increase. At one such session, youth players of various skill levels and ages took part in a coach-led demonstration while the coaches counted and took notes to the side. I paired players of similar ability levels with one another to ensure the quality was consistent and appropriate for that group.

What they found was that when players were given a ball and a specific skill or movement or passing pattern, and a clear demonstration of what was expected, players amassed more contacts on the ball in a shorter amount of time.

Players and coaches could see and experience how a series of turns, chops, or feints starts out unopposed – and in isolation – before we added factors such as increased speed, decreased rest periods, and eventually opposition or a game-like scenario to the movement.

Another example that is especially useful for young players is "chunking" or grouping a skill out over several sets. A simple yet ever-important skill such as juggles or one-touch per step dribbles performed for 100 repetitions could equal one set. Ten sets later, they would have 1,000 repetitions under their belt.

Performing a Cruyff turn, where each turn counts as a repetition to form sets, breaks the complexity down into manageable numbers. One of the best methods for accumulating functional and realistic touches on the ball comes in the form of passing against a wall or with a teammate. By adding passing – a necessary element of the game – players can work on different skills and rotate with each complete rep or set. This is how thousands of repetitions can accumulate in a short amount of time in a technical exercise, based first on proper technique and execution of the basics. Then, depending on what a player or coach sees, more advanced elements like the speed, weight, angle, and intensity of the passing – along with new variations such as taking one, two, three-touches before passing the ball back – can be added.

For the last 15 years, I have seen that the most challenging battle is often mental fatigue. Physically, the workouts can be taxing, but it is the mental endurance that gets stressed the most. This was true when I was a young player, and it is true now. Additionally, as a coach, it is immensely helpful to have experienced this approach firsthand. Returning back to educating other coaches on how best to present and approach this material, I always found importance in encouraging those willing and able to do a session themselves to do so.

As players improve and grow accustomed to the methodology, the workouts became faster, the movements became smoother, and the process is ramped-up. Additionally, aspects like creativity emerge with each workout. Improvisation is crucial for soccer, and it plays a major role in technical development and execution.

Ideally, what begins as a task becomes a lifestyle. Another key aspect of the methodology is that it encourages individuals to take an inventory of technical skills they need to perform in a session. Young players can use this structure and organization to help them plan their sessions and address their technical needs on their own time, which is the ultimate goal. This type of programming is similar to weight training where workouts, performed for sets and repetitions, are logged. For example, taking a tally of successful movements, passes completed, turns executed at speed, or three-touch (receive-manipulate-pass) sequences allow individuals to get a deeper understanding of what they are working on each session. Why is this important? If you ask a player or a coach, "What did you work on today?" the odds are you will get a general answer. "I worked on shooting and passing," or "We dribbled in a grid and did turns." I contend this type of recollection isn't good or detailed enough for players trying to push their abilities.

What is more helpful is when a player can confidently say something like, "I passed the ball 2,000 times today. I performed 200 Cruyff turns at speed. I received the ball 2,000 times because I passed it off a wall that many times. I dribbled at speed in a small grid for 30 seconds and touched the ball with every step. Then, I got sets of 50 juggles in ten times."

This level of specificity is valuable.

Make no mistake, the volume is intimidating on paper and it may be in practice. Most coaches and players need to begin with an example workout to help quell the doubts they may have about the method. Again, this is why I encourage coaches to design their own programs and try them on their own before introducing them to players. I also encourage players to create their own workouts and to reflect or even record that session a few times to document their progress.

Writing workouts and movements down also helps individuals design their sessions to target areas of their game that require the most focused work. By designing a workout filled with the necessary game-realistic movements, players and coaches can begin to think about what type of player they want to be or produce. Additionally, the process lends itself to reinforcing expectations and visualizing methods.

For many, the very thought of getting thousands of touches a day on the ball is unrealistic. And that is not unreasonable. This method is simple, but not easy. This approach is not for everyone. Some may simply lack the drive, skill, and access to an environment to reap the benefits from immersion-based training. Of course, some players – regardless of environment – will lack the internal drive and the capability to view challenges as opportunities for growth, rather than as insurmountable obstacles. This comes down to those with a fixed mindset versus those with a growth mindset. In her book, *Mindset – The New Psychology of Success*, Stanford psychologist Carol Dweck, Ph.D., discusses the differences of each mindset. In the book, Dweck's research highlights the simplest beliefs people have about themselves. Her findings indicate that how we view ourselves, and the tasks that lie before us, form our personality and differs based on two types of mindset.

A "fixed mindset" assumes that an individual's character, intelligence, and creative ability are static inputs, which cannot be changed in any meaningful way. Additionally, any success we experience is an affirmation of how those inherent factors measure up against an equally fixed standard. These people strive for success by avoiding failure at all costs as a way of maintaining their sense of being considered intelligent or skilled.

On the other hand, a "growth mindset" thrives on challenges and views failures not as a lack of intelligence or a deficiency, but as a motivating springboard and opportunity for growth. These people will aim to push the levels of their existing abilities to promote growth.

Dweck's research also points out that these two mindsets manifest from a very early age and affect a great deal of our behavior, including our relationships with others and ourselves. They help form how we view success and failure in sporting, professional, and even personal contexts. These mindsets ultimately help dictate our capacity for learning and how we seek happiness from the things we pursue.

Simplify the Structure

Individuals who undertake isolation training in any discipline showcase an uncanny ability to simplify their process. Breaking down a monumental task into micro-processes is paramount to success. One doesn't just learn to play an instrument or a new position in one session. The process takes dedicated allotments of time and energy.

Players deciding to accomplish 10,000 touches on the ball most days are driven, maybe even obsessed, about their pursuit of ball mastery. These are players willing to focus on single or grouped tasks for extended periods of time. They showcase a degree of mental endurance that outlasts others in their talent pools.

So, how is it that players can be developed and coaxed into subscribing to a concept emphasizing repetition *without turning them into robots*? If a player just decided to get 10,000 touches a day, would their brain turn to mush? Could this activity impede their development and extinguish their zest and motivation to play the game and have fun?

There is an entry fee associated with the programming here.

A major reality check that is also quite uncomfortable is that not every player is created equally. If a player is not inherently driven to take control and ownership over their development, the likelihood is that they will fizzle out after the first or second attempt. This is why it is important *not* to focus on the number 10,000 but to pick a manageable number to ensure quality over quantity.

A Means to an End

Individuals should attempt to draw meaning out of this program.

In addition to simplifying the process, eliminating excuses and distractions goes a long way toward building mental endurance and resilience in any discipline and pursuit.

Growing up, I didn't realize how lucky I was to have less. I grew up middle class without many of the conveniences we enjoy today. I didn't have a cell phone until I was 18-years-old, nor did I own a laptop until my second year at college.

Players are people. People get distracted. One of the major reasons people fail to meet goals in anything has less to do with motivation and more to do with accountability and ownership. Lasting progress and tangible results are generally the products of accountability and discipline. The willingness to log workouts, stick to a task, see a program to completion, and focus on something other than one's smartphone day after day is a major part of the equation. As such, keeping a training journal is *essential*.

Another part of shifting the training paradigm is making it entirely personal. When something is personal, it comes with a maturation process centered on paying attention to details. This means documenting and logging workouts and reflections to not only build a relationship with the ball, but also with oneself. Some days, players will not get anywhere near the number of touches they set as the goal. In fact, they will often fall short of the standard they set for themselves. It is at this point they can go back to their documentation, to their training journals or footage, and realistically and objectively see if that standard needs to change. But then again, on other days, they may smash through that ceiling.

In short, the fewer distractions and excuses a player has to contend with, the easier it becomes to find time to train and immerse themselves into a process.

Reality Checks

During my time in the Netherlands, I was told by both my teammates and coaches to focus heavily on getting extra work on the ball. And not just a few minutes here or there, but extra repetitions by the thousands. The two drivers for this requirement? One, I wasn't good enough. Two, the best players at the club I played with did this extra work as part of their daily life – and they were vying to be scouted by top academies, which are finishing schools of sorts for footballers. These institutions require players to have a baseline skillset mastered (and somewhat polished), so they can focus on accentuating and teaching other skills to talented players.

Empirical research in the case study conducted by the Journal of Sports Sciences, titled *Perceptual Skill in Soccer: Implications for Talent Identification and Development*, lends itself to reinforce the notion that over time, self-discovery, self-monitoring, and diligence became habitual. Perceptual skills like Recall Performance, Advance Cue Utilization, and Visual Search Strategy are integral to talent selection and development. Recall Performance is the ability to recover information related to football more effectively from one's memory. Advance Cue Utilization is classified as the ability to make precise predictions based on an opponent's posture and/or actions. Visual Search Strategy is centered on the ability to move the eyes continuously to focus on the important aspects of the game.[16]

Inevitably, the game changes as each generation gives way to the next. Soccer remains in constant flux with the passing of time, and players evolve with it. Playing styles shift with the ever-changing and popular philosophies of the day. As such, skillsets must keep pace with the game's dynamism. Players are assessed through their constant interaction with the ball and held to technical standards that may be different from previous generations. Positional play continues to shift the roles on the field, too. Defenders are expected to dictate play, midfielders are expected to interchange on-the-fly, outside backs operate as wingers, and goalkeepers in the modern game must be secure with the ball at their feet.

Additionally, the ability to process information and read the game in real-time on the field to make the correct decision, with or without the

[16] Williams, Andrew. (2000). Perceptual Skill in Soccer: Implications for Talent Identification and Development. *Journal of Sports Sciences*, **18**, 737-50, 10.1080/02640410050120113.

ball, at the right time, can indicate a player possesses high-level game intelligence.

Another reality check that every player must confront is the level of coaching they are exposed to throughout their formative years. Players will find themselves subjected to coaches whose goal is not to develop, but rather to *win* at all costs.

The youth game is where fundamental skills and habit formation should be strengthened, but anyone who has witnessed the youth game outside of the professional academy environment knows that what is valued and coached is very different from what is preached. To this end, individual supplemental training is essential.

CHAPTER 6: INSIDE THE CAULDRON OF ADVANCED PLAYER DEVELOPMENT

Motivation is the spark that ignites the fire.
Discipline is the fuel to keep that fire going.

Author Unknown

For the truly dedicated, the pursuit of mastery – the constant unglamorous work performed for years – is the reward. That pursuit tends to separate people by testing one's ability and willingness to work toward an objective more frequently, with greater focus, and for a longer period of time.

The idea of a player willing to do targeted work, in isolation (when no one is watching), is common in sport. There is an idealization of the motif of an individual who works themselves to the top levels *away* from the spotlight, but it is also *the reality* of the journey.

The work and commitment required to excel are only two of many factors that help determine success for an individual. Players who put in the time to work on their game, beyond just showing up to team training sessions, have an edge over those whose perception of hard work is not wired into their mindset. What a player on a dedicated and persistent development path sees as valuable supplemental work, others see as a thousand thankless tasks.

The challenge is finding the appropriate way for players *to identify* the areas in which they need to improve. Another element that helps optimize key processes of development is keeping an actual record of the work performed over time. This can take the form of diligently recording personal data sets (workout logs) – a psychosocial skill. The modern player also has the technological advantage of using resources in the digital space – recording and uploading their workouts for further analysis and feedback, and they are ultimately able to assess their progress through objective means at regular intervals. This may all seem overly analytical, but a high level of attention to detail is required if we want a better objective understanding of skillsets and a player's training habits.

The research paper *Toward a Grounded Theory of the Psychosocial Competencies and Environmental Conditions Associated with Soccer Success,*[17] written by researchers Nicholas Holt and John Dunn from the University of Alberta, explores the major psychosocial competencies associated with soccer success during adolescence.

The study tracked 40 participants, of which 20 were Canadian international youth players (with an average age of 16.8 years), 14 were English professional youth players (with an average age of 16.2 years), and six were English professional coaches.

The research identified four major psychosocial competencies that seem crucial to success in elite youth development.

1. **Discipline:** the ability to display appropriate discipline and dedicated behaviors (conforming dedication to the sport, a willingness to make sacrifices…).
2. **Commitment:** the motivational forces (love of the game, determination to succeed, social status, ability to set career planning goals) and sport-based objectives (playing up, gaining exposure…) of young players.
3. **Resilience:** the ability to bounce back after adversity using coping mechanisms.
4. **Social support:** the ability to perceive and use available sources to gain emotional, informational, and tangible support.

In the context of player development, a common belief is that 'driven' players are born and not made. As subjective and circumstantial as that premise is, by studying the game from a tactical, sociological, and anthropological standpoint, it is possible to construct a better picture of the primary factors that influence the major roles in player development.

From an environmental perspective, systems that place a high value on small-sided games require different skillsets to systems that play on bigger pitches. Players who play in smaller areas at a younger age receive more contact with the ball and experience more game actions each outing. In other words, there is a greater frequency of duels, attacking and defensive opportunities, positional interchange, and more chances to be creative or unpredictable on the ball. Additionally, these environments also exhibit a level of play with higher baseline technical

---

[17] Holt, N., & Dunn, J. (2010). Toward a Grounded Theory of the Psychosocial Competencies and Environmental Conditions Associated with Soccer Success. *Journal of Applied Sport Psychology*, September 2004, 199-219, 10.1080/10413200490437949.

skill levels (such as the ability to pass, dribble, shoot, and receive the ball with success), and tend to produce players who have more versatility, higher confidence on the ball, and better body literacy compared to environments with lesser skill levels. Here, players can test their skills more frequently without a dramatic drop-off in the level of play.

Another component is how a player is influenced by their environment. For example, if the game is accessible in a variety of social settings (e.g., with pals in the park), players will develop in informal, unstructured environments as well as hyper-organized and highly-structured coached settings with a team. They will get the best of both worlds.

On a more technical level, the frequency of touches on the ball in small-sided games can be high as passing skills (circulation and recirculation), defending (regaining possession), and attacking scenarios (such as one-on-one dribbling and defending opportunities) increase due to the confined space. The requisite technical ability of each player demands quick interplay, comfort, and confidence on the ball, and, of course, creativity!

I contend that players need to not only perform but excel within a system on a *consistent* basis if they are to drastically improve to the level where they can make development-based leaps. Those players that shine in each of the psychosocial competencies – discipline, commitment, resilience, and social support – along with their associated subcategories, tend to do best.

Exploring the Psychosocial Skills

Framing the context of each psychosocial competency with real-world examples is essential to better understand their importance and application to player development.

Discipline

With regards to discipline, the research indicated that professional and international soccer environments and organizations impose strict institutional demands in terms of lifestyle and training on young players. As a result of these demands, players learned to display appropriately disciplined and dedicated behaviors on and off the field.

Conforming dedication is a subcategory of discipline that represents the ways in which young players comply with institutional demands presented to them. For example, players in the study demonstrated observable levels of dedication both in their personal lives and soccer performances by following club and team rules. They also applied taught concepts without argument, and progressed through their ability to take personal responsibility for their development and the outcomes associated with their decisions.

Personal responsibility is a subcategory in which players in high-level development environments differ greatly from players in less competitive environments. For example, in high-level settings, players understood that coaches expected them to be personally responsible for their own development and behavior. The fact they were surrounded by equally if not superiorly-skilled players underlined the reality that they could be replaced at a moment's notice for failure to comply. Such a cauldron of development puts the onus on the player (and not the coach) to improve themselves as responsible individuals.

Examples include training on weaknesses or deficient areas of their game without direct prompts and supervision from coaches, being on-time to training, and having a professional approach to their conduct at all times.

In high-level environments, those players actively seeking additional training opportunities showed an individual desire to improve by processing and applying the feedback received from the coaching staff to improve specific areas of their game.

The personal responsibility attribute empowers players to assume control of their individual development (as the coach develops the collective/team) and also applies to behaviors off the field.

The ability to follow direct instruction is also a key element to a player's success. Players who follow directions effectively are easier to train. Coaches often assess how "coachable" a player is, and it should serve as no surprise that players who can process what is being asked of them, and translate it into positive performances, have a higher chance of making it at the higher levels of soccer.

One of the coaches interviewed in the case study said, "As a football club, we try not to put up with any sort of nonsense. From 9 to 16 years old, you do as you are told, and if anybody steps out of line we won't sign them, because it's just a hassle that you don't need."

A similar point was relayed by a player at a professional club in England, interviewed in the study, who stated, "They pay my wages, they tell me what to do. They tell you to play wide, or play sweeper, you do it to the best of your ability."

High-level players are required to produce **dominant** performances that align with a desired outcome in competitive settings. Coaches prioritize a player's performance to assess progress. Players can train more often, and with better methods, but ultimately, it is game performance that is most crucial. Soccer is a results-based industry.

Players must learn to do the simple things well. Coaches love displays of skill, but more than anything, they value consistency. Doing the simple things to perfection is king. For example, a defender that defends efficiently, or a winger that can deliver quality service over and over, may be better indicators of competent players than someone who produces flash-in-the-pan audacious displays of skill and trickery. Much of this relates to team-based game models. The majority of required game actions are tactical assignments and decisions made in unison... influenced by a system. Creativity and flashes of skill are necessary, but not at the expense of tactical discipline and consistency.

Commitment

Committed players show a willingness to sacrifice valued elements of adolescent life to pursue a professional career in soccer. These sacrifices are seen as an expected and required part of elite development tracks in world soccer. These sacrifices include reduced time with family and friends, and a limited social life. Life for the majority of pro-track players involves training when others are not.

One particular youth player discussed the importance of getting one extra structured training session a week with the youth teams and reserves of his professional club, or with other teams in an unofficial capacity – even in the off-season – because he saw it as getting 52 more training sessions than his peers and opposition in each year.

Time spent away from immediate family is a common sacrifice that elite players make. Often, this stems from additional training opportunities that take players away from family events and activities. Another decision awaiting players is moving away from home at a young age to immerse themselves in a high-level training environment. This may mean moving to a foreign country where the individual has little familiarity or knowledge of cultures, languages, and customs outside of the club setting. Such a willingness to sacrifice at young ages have a profound effect on an individual's personal development away from sport.

Elite players also sacrifice time spent with their peers. Similar to sacrificing time away from their families, players motivated by success in the game often forgo recreational experiences in their emerging social life; instead, they opt to play matches and train more frequently. A life dictated by early nights, foregoing social outings with friends, and even earlier mornings to train, defines a young player's life on the elite track.

These types of sacrifices relate to a sense of delayed gratification, the realization that rewards are not gained instantly (but in the future).

Researchers also found a player's motives for prioritizing their development aligned with planned career goals associated with soccer. Although they played for the love of the game, elite players displayed an unyielding determination to succeed. Many were also driven by the perceived social status gained from earning a living as a top footballer. In the context of this book, players tend to play for the love of the game because the game functions as a primary formative activity that helps *define their identity*. Driven players often describe themselves by what they excel at, or would like to achieve. Additionally, the truly dedicated individuals accumulate the most time pursuing that which continually intrigues them. In other words, they make sacrifices because more training will make them better, and they know the pay-off comes in the form of a possible professional career.

Perhaps the biggest driver related to commitment is the determination to succeed at all costs. This is what separates players within a player pool. Players striving to be their very best train harder, more often, and willingly seek out chances to play up a level or age group to gain exposure. The mindset associated with players determined to succeed at all costs is geared toward seeking challenges.

Playing against peers of lesser skill does not appeal to the truly elite players. They want to test themselves against the best available competition while understanding they may not win or dominate for long periods of time (delayed gratification). However, the probability of improvement over time makes the commitment worthwhile.

In many cases, playing up expedites overall skill development and tactical understanding as the benefits of playing against better players provides insight into what the next level looks, plays, and feels like. Additionally, players gain exposure by playing up, by gaining access to superior training methods in high-class facilities from high-quality coaches.

Resilience

The capacity to be resilient, here, relates to the ability to rebound positively after a setback. More to the point, a resilient player displays the aptitude to overcome personal and contextual obstacles and embraces adversity.

Resilience requires positive coping responses to manage the demands of the game at the higher levels.

Players face a myriad of obstacles they must overcome. One of the most common is parental pressure. The expectations of parents are often unrealistic and far from attainable. The high emotional investment weighs heavy on associations, and when these interactions are mismanaged, they will strain development and relationships.

However, the absence of pressure can be detrimental to development too. At serious levels, the game *has to matter*. The consequences of poor performance can be quite steep. The game offers no shortage of teachable moments and lessons. For the parent, finding the right balance between encouragement, influence, and guidance is paramount.

Obstacles, like injury, lack of form, exposure to bad coaches and methods, and emotional challenges, can be overwhelming experiences. Every high-level player experiences each of these resilience-testing aspects over the course of their journey.

The difference is that top players use situational coping strategies to help manage the pressures of their involvement in elite soccer environments. According to the research, players echo what coaches present such as the importance of responding positively to challenges. Another coping strategy involves participants acknowledging the importance of having the confidence to thrive on pressure *instead* of seeing it as a limitation.

Players who train and play with high-intensity methods in high-stakes environments will make mistakes. Others will constantly challenge them. It is up to the individual to learn how to positively learn from these encounters. A top player must be able to react appropriately to mistakes, negative performances, and blunt criticism.

Success in elite environments is hinged upon one's ability to cope with pressure. Adaptation to change and learning to better understand is part of the equation. The other part is using pressure as fuel to gain experience. The best players in any sport have short-term memories and are less affected by mistakes. For example, a misplaced pass, a shot that sails over the goal, a string of defeats, and setbacks on and off the field may seem significant at the time – but they can be converted to learning opportunities.

Social Support

Players possessing an ability to use available social support systems are able to overcome obstacles more easily. According to research conducted by Carolyn Cutrona and Daniel Russell[18], players often benefit from three different types of social support: emotional, informational, and tangible.

Within the context of Cutrona and Russell's research, the single most important providers of social support are parents. However, the respective support functions performed by mothers and fathers differ. Naturally, people require emotional support. Having someone to turn to for comfort, to confide in, and share thoughts and feelings with – well, they are the foundations of a trustworthy relationship. Support of this nature can come from either parent; however, research indicates the mother usually serves as the primary source of emotional support.

Informational or experiential support generally originates with the father, in soccer development case studies, although that is likely to change as the women's game continues to succeed and remain popular. Fathers with the experience of playing soccer, and institutional knowledge of the game, may better understand the importance and demands of high-level training applications in soccer-specific pursuits. Again, this is not to say a mother with similar soccer experience cannot serve in this capacity; she most certainly can with great success. The cautionary element with informational support is the chance of relationship strain if the information shared, and the experiences relayed from parent to child, do not resonate or apply to specific situations.

The last component is tangible support, which often manifests in parents providing the financial means and backing for expenses associated with playing competitive soccer. These costs extend into paying for private lessons, securing additional training opportunities, private counseling with sports psychologists, paying for gym memberships, and paying for tournaments, travel, equipment, attire, and beyond. Although not every player has parents who possess the means to fund as much of their development as possible, it is seen as a social advantage.

In the next chapter, we will explore the leap from good to great, and discuss the outlier effect in technical skill development.

---

[18] Cutrona, C. E., & Russell, D. W. (1990). Type of social support and specific stress: Toward a theory of optimal matching. In B. R. Sarason, I. G. Sarason, & G. R. Pierce (Eds.), Wiley series on personality processes. *Social support: An interactional view* (p. 319–366). John Wiley & Sons.

CHAPTER 7: FROM GOOD TO GREAT

What happens when results matter in the youth game more than any other factor? What kind of player emerges from a system that reduces everything into two categories: wins and losses?

One might think such a system produces ruthless competitors with elite skill development capabilities and an insatiable desire to crush the competition. One might think that this system produces the best players on the planet.

Errr... no.

The problem with focusing development on a results-based outcome is that the approach emphasizes *the outcome* over *the process*. In 2011, FC Barcelona was on top of world football in terms of a philosophy of play and results (both domestically and in Europe). The players responsible for the magic on the pitch, such as Lionel Messi, Xavi Hernández, Andrés Iniesta, Pedro, Sergio Busquets, Thiago, Carles Puyol, Cesc Fàbregas, Víctor Valdés, and Gerard Piqué, emerged from a system at the club's academy, *La Masia*. Each product of the academy possessed the skill to be a star as an individual. However, these players also understood how to operate as a team as they had been allowed to do so at the youth levels for years. That same year, in an interview with *The Guardian*, Xavi described the difference between Barcelona and other teams.

"Some youth academies worry about winning; we worry about education. You see a kid who lifts his head up, who plays the pass first time, pum, and you think, 'Yep, he'll do.' Bring him in, coach him. Our model was imposed by [Johan] Cruyff; it's an Ajax model."

The importance of learning and actual skill development over wins and losses seems quite simple. However, the framework of a club or culture must accommodate such an approach without placing too much importance on youth results. Ironically, a process that allows players to focus on developing their technical and tactical ability – over all else – tends to produce outright winners at the older ages where results should matter more.

Compare such an approach that exists not only at Barcelona, but at top clubs in other countries as well, to the system present in the United States. In the U.S., what drives the youth game has often (and historically) been league standings and win/loss records as evaluative methods rather than skill-based accomplishments and competencies.

Factors such as a lack of a true soccer culture, pay-to-play, competition with other youth sports and activities, and a rather fragmented organization of the sport – from the top-down – play major roles in prioritizing results over development. As such, quality is primarily determined by wins and losses and less by technical and tactical skills mastered, concepts learned, and abilities. These factors are key drivers that deprioritize skill in favor of results.

These problems are realities in many countries. In places where coaching education remains costly, there exists a disconnect and a lack of oversight from the concepts taught in courses being performed on the training field to those taking place on match day. In other words, youth teams are geared towards training to win at all costs. This approach shifts the playing paradigm. For example, absent a culture that allows for development over results, young players are *less likely* to go out and play unstructured soccer unless there are rewards (in the form of parental and coaching praise, scholarships to a university, and winning trophies).

There is no getting away from the fact that producing technically proficient players requires patience, persistence, and a great deal of time and immersion dedicated toward specific tasks. This is why the very thought, let alone the actual practice of accumulating thousands of repetitions a day, is physically draining and mentally exhausting for the casual player – especially in the absence of a system that accepts that skill development and learning should matter over results.

Immersive Learning

Success in sport requires deep immersion in game-realistic training environments for prolonged periods of time. The aim and learning objective is to reach peak performance levels of a specific skill with a high level of repeatability with variables factored in, most notably the presence of an opposing team. Such an approach must be sustainable, and it must push the player's ability to the point where they are challenged and see the value in the nuances of a training scheme.

The key training point here is players must be afforded the bandwidth to play and focus on repeating the activity *with consistency* to drive performance levels, no matter how infinitesimal the details may seem.

For example, at elite levels, a player with the ability to receive a ball, shift it away from a pressing opponent, and deliver a pass to the correct foot at the correct speed to a teammate with situational proficiency, is indicative of a player taking isolated movements – trained and rehearsed in game-realistic scenarios – and executing the sequence to a point approaching mastery.

In that same interview with *The Guardian*, Xavi discussed the importance and role of the rondo as a training guide and framework for the overarching philosophy of play at the club.

"It's all about rondos [piggy in the middle]. Rondo, rondo, rondo. Every. Single. Day. It's the best exercise there is. You learn responsibility and not to lose the ball. If you lose the ball, you go in the middle. Pum-pum-pum-pum, always one touch."

He goes on to stress the importance of technical ability by stating, "I like the fact that talent, technical ability, is valued above physical condition now. I'm glad that's the priority; if it wasn't, there wouldn't be the same spectacle."

Focusing on the micro-process of a larger playing framework can lead to a positive outcome. Immersion training allows players to have short-term memories on the field regarding mistakes and miscues because the training environment is not punitive. Instead, the training environment should encourage players to be creative, to take risks, and to be bold with their play.

Average vs. Elite

A main difference between average and elite player development is not necessarily the skills one acquires in development, but *the application* of those skills in meaningful competition against quality opposition.

In one case study, researchers found that the skills required during game performance were defined as the ability of an individual player to perform the right action at the right moment, and quickly adapt to new configurations of play and the circulation of the ball.[19]

The study states, "For a player to perform the right action at the right moment, with a successful performance or outcome, a proper understanding of the game is required. Hence, besides well-developed physiological and technical characteristics, elite players also need well-developed tactical skills (French & Thomas, 1987; Helsen & Starkes, 1999; Nougier & Rossi, 1999; Starkes, 1987; Williams, Davids, Burwitz,

---

[19] **Kannekens, R., Elferink-Gemser, M.T., & Visscher, C. (2009).** Tactical skills of world-class soccer teams. *Journal of Sport Sciences*, 27(8), 807-812.

& Williams, 1993). This applies especially to players of invasion games such as soccer, in which players compete on the same field of action as their opponents. Because the environment in these games changes constantly, decisions must be made quickly and accurately, requiring good tactical skills."

This point reinforces the need for players to be afforded the opportunities to learn and develop technically and tactically in systems that prioritize learning over winning at younger ages. As such, tying the importance of immersive technical training requires advanced tactical levels and training. This concept is present in sports outside football, such as tennis, baseball, ice hockey, and basketball, to name but a few.

To take some examples, elite basketball players shoot hundreds of free throws or jump shots a week to the point of perfection. Elite tennis players hone a technical skill – such as a serve – by practicing for hours during training to help automate the movement and process. Baseball players take batting practice for hours on end to improve the timing, hand-eye coordination, and swing technique they will have to repeat in a game.

These technical micro-processes – the manner in which the best players break down each game movement in a tactical sense – sheds light on how athletes outside soccer share a common method and approach to improve. Perhaps this is one example of the difference between how an average or good player trains and prepares, versus the approaches and application of an elite player. When I attended the University of Kentucky, one of college basketball's perennial powerhouses, I watched some of the best players – most with the potential to reach the NBA – train like men possessed.

The basketball team at Kentucky, much like other elite basketball programs, exists in a vacuum that prepares players for professional basketball. Seldom was there a time when I was at the recreation center and gym for the general student population that I wouldn't see a Kentucky player practicing an aspect of his game for hours. As a collegiate athlete myself, I knew a visit to the campus rec center usually indicated an athlete sought out extra training. Most Division I athletes dedicate enough time in specialized training complexes and gyms for our respective teams.

Additionally, being a student-athlete can place an individual in a perpetual state of physical and mental exhaustion. This is why, late at night and early each morning during my offseason, I would see members of the basketball team meander into the rec center and practice free throws, three-point shots, and jump shots to exhaustion, often before or after their 'official' team practice.

Big-time collegiate programs in the U.S. recruit the best-in-breed and place them in state-of-the-art facilities. It doesn't take a genius to understand why these basketball players trained with intensity in a variety of environments. Even though they already made it to a premier collegiate program on full scholarships, the basketball players, like all elite players, trained to compete at their current level while *preparing themselves for the next level.*

As players at the top of their game, they devoted hundreds of hours doing the simple things well, homing in on effective processes to the point of perfection. To be elite in any discipline, especially football, individuals on that specific path understand that their ability to perform with consistency at high levels comes only from investing large amounts of additional time in these specific tasks.

Finding the Right Key

Athletics, arts, and academia all require a similarly rigorous approach in pursuit of skill acquisition and performance mastery. I interviewed Young Hee Park recently, and she is a faculty member of the Midwest Conservatory of Music near Chicago, in addition to the American Music Institute. Young is a professional pianist originally from South Korea who holds a Master's Degree and Performer's Certificate in Piano Performance from Northern Illinois University, and is a sought-after musician for professional performances requiring an expert pianist.

Her journey typifies the route that great writers, athletes, artists, and of course, musicians take from beginner to advanced status.

"When I first started playing, I was nine-years-old, and I practiced for maybe one hour a day. My teacher in South Korea taught me to focus on the parts I struggled with over and over. If I did not play a part perfectly, I would spend most of the hour playing that specific part over and over until it was perfect."

Young's journey, however, sheds light on something that's often overlooked regarding skill-acquisition with repetition.

"As I got older, I learned to teach others. When I was more advanced, I learned to practice the difficult parts of a composition and connect them with other difficult parts. When I become an "advanced" pianist, I practiced for over three hours a day. In music, like all art forms, the better a person is at something, the longer they have to train. It does no good for a professional pianist to train for only one hour. The music and movements become more demanding, and I must spend hours repeating the complex parts. So, the better I get, the more I have to train and repeat the musical movements."

Much like music, acquiring technical mastery in football may require players to train to the point of mental and physical exhaustion. They must focus on the little things they don't quite do well at first. True progression is impossible without mastery of the basic movements and skills.

It is this level of mastery and command of the basics that connects football to music and other art forms. Even as a professional pianist with the ability to compose and understand music theory, Young rehearses and plays basic scales and progressions daily to prepare her for more complex movements.

For Young, no shortcuts exist on the pathway to becoming a professional. The art of persistence differentiates the average player from the elite in both football and music. As a top-level musician who runs a successful music school out of her home, she is not exempt from training the basics. For over 20 years, she practices scales from five to seven o'clock every morning, starting with the basics. As a mother of two children, she devotes her efforts to the task of *perfecting* what she already knows how to do (simple scales and progressions) to extend her ability through deep practice.

So, what applications translate to soccer development? In many ways, Young practices piano like great footballers practice their trade because for talents such as these to be realized, rehearsal, training, and performance must become their lifestyle. To them, training their skills are as normal as starting the car or getting dressed. To a young player or musician, this can prove to be extremely challenging as the cultural aspect must reinforce the lessons derived from the training.

"With my students in America, they avoid the challenging parts of the piano. They tell me they understand, but their play says otherwise. In other countries, even in South Korea, the best students, artists, and musicians do not hide from the challenging part. They work and work at it until it's no longer considered 'the challenging part' of the piece. Then, they move on and learn a more complicated piece. This is how musicians go from beginner to good, good to great, great to advanced levels."

Exploring the Outlier Effect

A persistence-based approach is not for everyone. Dedicated athletes, musicians, and artists tend to take an obsessive approach to honing their craft. Society conditions people to covet the results without engaging in an immersive process. In other words, we want the best results in the least amount of time.

Persistence training can aid in positive habit formation. Additionally, this specific training methodology has less to do with genetics and athleticism and more to do with individuals combining the skill they possess with graft, persistence, and dedication to separate themselves from the pack.

Deep practice can strengthen a player's foundational skillset. One major benefit to deep practice for footballers is it allows them to explore the depths of their abilities at length, to the point they become so good at the simple things that they can reproduce the skill successfully with consistency. Additionally, by improving their technical level, players can perform more complex movements and skills.

Perhaps the most observable instances of deep practice take place before the game. Regardless of the sport, the crowd can watch how repetition and immersion training manifest before the competition starts. During the warm-up, in particular, it is possible to observe how each player cycles through the micro-processes specific to their position. To the untrained eye, it may be less obvious. However, the processes on display are those belonging to outliers.

Watch the athletes do the little things – the five-yard passes, receiving a pass and accelerating for the first six or seven yards. Taking part in a shooting activity with precision. A professional player's first touch, a basketball player's repetitive jump shots from the perimeter, or the control of a quarterback's passes to players running routes – these are the simple, but not easy, activities performed at the highest level.

Another quality the outlier athlete possesses is intentionality. Elite players do not take pot shots on goal before matches. Professional quarterbacks do not throw the ball as hard as they can trying to look spectacular. Great point guards are not practicing elaborate tricks that do not lend themselves to practical game movements.

Instead, these athletes focus on perfecting the little things. The elite player analyzes the scenarios that unfold before them at high speeds. *That* is a skill.

In an interview with CNN's Anderson Cooper, the author of the bestselling book, *Outliers*, Malcolm Gladwell spoke about the requisite number of hours (amount of time) before a person can reach a level considered mastery. The conversation was fascinating in that its logic applies directly to player development in football.

Naturally, players, parents, and coaches want prompt results with their training methods. Society at large is addicted to instant, overnight change. The dangers in applying this to technical development revolve around the lack of dedicated consistency to a given training method.

There are a few constants in drawing parallels between the 10,000 hour theory and getting upwards of 10,000 touches a day on the ball: dedicated time to the activity (specialization) and consistency. Like a conventional job where an employee trades time for dollars, specialization training requires a player to trade time for skill acquisition and eventually mastery.

> **Anderson Cooper:** And you talk about this 10,000 hour rule, that it's not just a matter of well, this person's a genius, has amazing ability, it's actual practice and hard work.
>
> **Malcolm Gladwell:** So a bunch of, a group of really brilliant psychologists in the field of "expertise research" sat down and tried to figure out: "How long do you have to work at something before you become really good?" And the answer seems to be, it's an extraordinarily consistent answer in an incredible number of fields that is you need to have practiced, to have apprenticed, for 10,000 hours before you get good. So, every great classical composer without exception, composed for at least 10 years before they write their masterwork."
>
> **AC:** Mozart is composing at ten…
>
> **MG:** Mozart is composing at eleven, but he's composing garbage at 11. I mean, he doesn't produce something great until he's 22 or 23. Concerto No. 9-271… If I asked you, "How long did it take for you, when you were doing this job, before you were comfortable, good at what you're doing?…"
>
> **AC:** Ten years, at least…

MG: Same with me. It's an incredibly consistent finding. It's really important because it says, "We are far too impatient with people. When we assess whether someone has got what it takes to do a certain job, we always want to make that assessment after six months or a year. That's ridiculous. The kinds of jobs we have people do today are sufficiently complex and they require a long time to reach mastery. What we should be doing is setting up institutions and structures that allow people to spend the time and effort to reach mastery. Not judging them prematurely."

AC: What is the takeaway? What's the lesson for people who want to be more successful? I mean, in some ways, it is good news they don't have to be geniuses.

MG: I'm very anxious that this book not be seen as a self-help book, but be seen as a kind of community health book. Because what I really want people to do is start thinking about, "How can we as a society build institutions that provide opportunities to work hard?"

Technical Takeaways

Regarding player development and skill acquisition, timeframes are essential. The human body has a limited window to perform at optimal levels. A player just learning the game at seven or eight years of age will most likely not have reached mastery levels by the time they're 18-years old, but they should be well on their way. Additionally, many of the best players at the pinnacle of the game's talent pools are professionals, or at the very least, on-track to become professionals by the time they are 18 or 19-years old.

A technical takeaway here is that players engaging in ball mastery methods, including getting 10,000 touches a day, will not necessarily produce a professional player. It will, however, produce a technically proficient player *if* that training has been in the right context and with a supportive yet competitive environment that constantly allows that player to push the limits of their skills.

Those that go on to play at the top levels combine their skill with other attributes, competencies, and circumstances as they continue to develop. Technical ability is but one area where players must be exceptional to succeed at *their* highest levels. Players should strive to become outliers in their proximal talent pools. The appropriate environment and competition, combined with proper coaching, can shape a player's fate before a ball is even kicked.

The outlier has developed the skill to reduce and eventually eliminate distractions. They can also focus on the mental and physical rigors of persistence training consistently over time, more often and for longer durations, than many of their peers.

CHAPTER 8: A GAME HIDDEN IN PLAIN SIGHT

During my first few years playing collegiate soccer, I used to go running on Chicago's lakefront path, in-season, as a way to keep fit and – quite frankly – to clear my head.

If you have never been on the lakefront path, it's something uniquely Chicagoan. On the one side, Lake Michigan's waves crash against the city's edge, and on the other lies the magnificent urban sprawl – a jagged smile of concrete and steel jutting out of the ground to the sky. Nestled neatly within that jagged smile was an urban soccer league playing under the floodlights near North Avenue Beach. I often stopped to watch the teams play at my turnaround point to head back to Chicago's South Loop.

One Sunday morning, the day after a tough collegiate game, I went for a run from campus to the lakefront path to loosen up my legs and shake out the contusions from the previous night's exertions. As I ran by the fields where a game was being played, a stray ball crossed the path. Without breaking my stride, I instinctually hit a low, driven ball back to the field and continued on my run. One of the players let out a sharp whistle to get my attention. I pointed to my chest – you mean *me*? – and the players nodded and waved at me to approach the field.

Startled, I shook my head and thought there was no way I was going to tangle with a random men's league. For starters, it was an NCAA violation and secondly, I didn't want to get snapped by some clumsy hack of a player. I jogged over to a nearby water fountain to get a drink and heard the approaching click-clack of boot studs on pavement grow louder and louder. I turned just in time to see that player who whistled at me running up.

He said, "We need an extra player." Studying me for a moment before continuing, he added, "You want to play? You like soccer, yes?" in a prominent Polish-American accent.

"I can play, but..."

Before I could finish my sentence, he ushered me onto the turf field and whistled sharply again, signaling for a little boy to run up and hand me a jersey. I peered down at the kid who held the jersey up to me patiently before shaking it, inviting me to grab it. The boy, who looked to be about ten-years-old and sounded distinctly different to the first player, said, "My dad wants you to play on his team. Put this on; I'll hold your shirt for you."

Taking stock of the situation, I thought about what might happen if I got hurt or caught playing in non-NCAA competition in-season. The players waited while I retied my running shoes. For a few moments, I murmured to myself, "What are you doing?" Naturally, the stand-in referee objected to my random inclusion, and the opposing team swarmed him and argued. After a back-and-forth exchange in Polish, the ref relented.

Did I want to play? Absolutely, and in hindsight, there was no way I was going to turn down playing. I slotted in as a holding midfielder. I expected the first few minutes to be typical men's league chaos – players passing the ball behind the intended target foot, guys dribbling when they should pass, tackles flying in from behind, lovely stuff.

I kept my mouth shut and played simple, reverting back to my days playing pick-up games. Less thinking, more playing.

But this was a different brand of the game. I set up a goal and cracked a shot off the post from twenty-five yards out, and the pace of play picked up. This was nothing like I predicted. The players were technically sound. There was an assortment of younger players who did the running, tackling, and tracking – myself included. The experience was important because, as a college player, in a condensed and busy sporting and academic schedule, downtime is valuable.

The truth was, for me, that college soccer was great, especially at the Division I level, but this was a different type of game. It was considerably more technical, and the competition was excellent. It was obvious many of these men had played at a reasonably high level, perhaps even abroad.

For me, the college game was as close as I would get to playing professionally. In more than a few ways, it placed similar demands on the athlete and afforded unique opportunities, too. For starters, it allowed players to travel the country, get outfitted like a professional player, and play scrimmages and friendlies against professional teams as tune-ups.

However, the reality is college soccer is the pinnacle for most American players. At the Division I level, the game is predicated on athleticism and power. This is not to say the modern college game isn't technical, it definitely is, but the condensed three-to-four month season morphs the game into a very "American" game – lots of kicking, running, and hitting.

After the game in the park, the guys on the team patted me on the head and welcomed me to partake in the post-game pleasantries. We walked over to the sidelines, where the families clapped and shouted at each other in a bilingual exchange. An ice chest was wheeled out, and the kids handed every player a Stiegl beer. I thought about declining the drink, but I did not want to insult these guys, so I cracked open the can and clinked with them. I exchanged numbers with the captain, whose family gave me a ride back to campus. I was pretty happy about the whole thing, too, because I knew I had found something invaluable – *an opportunity hidden in plain sight.*

The perks, for a 19-year-old collegiate player, were fantastic. I would get to play at night, I got free beer, and these guys had no interest in telling the NCAA about my rogue participation in their league, nor did they care. They simply wanted me to play.

This meant I would get high-level team training with my college team; I would be able to lift and run and optimize my conditioning with the advantage of having access to state-of-the-art facilities and a highly-dedicated staff of trainers, strength and conditioning coaches, and of course, the actual coaching team. But I also knew I would get something more – playing time and minutes – something I was finding elusive on the collegiate front. The thing about the college season is how compressed it is, and if you're out of form, injured, or the team is playing well without you, or the coach is set on one rotation, the chances to make an impact are drastically minimized.

Finding this urban night league meant that for every collegiate game I saw little-to-no time in, I was getting ridiculously valuable game experience with the Polish team. Soon, I found that some of these extremely talented immigrant players found obscure work in the city, which meant the lineups frequently changed (some guys often left to find work elsewhere and never returned). After a month, I enjoyed playing with this team over the university team.

With these players, many of whom played at a very high level, my personality and identity as a player matured. These were men with families, jobs, and obligations that extended beyond the pitch, and yet their intensity and passion for playing remained high. For me, this was an important step in my maturation process as both a player and as a young man. The entire experience helped me find a different version of the game that I could tap into on a regular basis.

The opportunity, for me, was fantastic. Because I played consistently with the Polish team, it tremendously helped my college game. Not only was I getting about two hours of training with the college team per day, but I was getting an additional two or three games with the Polish team at least three nights a week. Personally, I believe *the game* is the most important teacher, and logging minutes of dedicated game time definitely sharpens a player's decision-making and gives them experience and high-level, game-realistic repetitions on the ball, and in scenarios with game-realistic consequences.

Deliberate Play

According to *The Role of Deliberate Practice in the Acquisition of Expert Performance* (Anders Ericsson, et al.), that well-known study which popularized the 10,000-hour theory, "The domain-specific nature of experts' superior performance implies that acquired knowledge and skill are important to the attainment of expert performance."

If one was to apply this theory of deep practice to soccer, the condition should be that a player must possess, at minimum, a basic level of acquired knowledge and skill in soccer. This basic, entry skill level and understanding are necessary to potentially pursue a path of what is considered the execution of expert performance. In other words, one should approach the concept armed with a baseline ability to play the game at the very least; a basic technical level on a player-by-player and environment-by-environment basis.

The same case study goes on to state, "Superior performance by very young children without prior instruction may suggest exceptional promise, leading to the early onset of training. This, in turn, leads to a consistently greater accumulation of practice relative to later-start individuals." What this means (or should mean) is that there are players who exhibit a seemingly "natural" ability to absorb concepts and execute them with a greater frequency of success early-on. Moreover, the earlier a player accomplishes this, the more likely they will accumulate a greater level of ability and skill-based execution to build-on and reinforce their level when compared with those who are introduced to the activity, and acquire skill, later in their development.

In soccer, the concept of deep practice is similar to the discipline of competitive weight lifting, running, swimming, and even archery. Success is achieved through discipline and consistency. Discipline in this sense can be classified, or thought of, as doing what you're supposed to do, when you're supposed to do it, with consistency over a long timeframe. A variable here is the idea of burnout associated with mental, physical, and emotional fatigue, which could lead to quitting the game entirely.

Once a player starts to disregard training on their own and playing in a variety of environments, they begin to form a habit of quitting when things don't appeal to them. Once consistency and discipline toward a task or skill wane, it becomes easier to quit – I classify this as "negative habit formation," and this is often the difference between a pretender and a serious player. The willingness to work towards an attainable and measurable goal on a consistent basis equates to completing more sessions that mirror meaningful competition match play, and which stress the skills needed in that meaningful competition.

Interpretations and Criticisms

Shortly after writing about the 10,000-touches-a-day concept for *These Football Times* and *The Guardian*, I received an abundance of feedback from coaches, players, parents, and interested readers. It's irresponsible to make the assertion that a player who does any *one* thing for an extended period of time will 'make it' in the game, and that applies to getting 10,000 functional touches a day on the ball.

Some of the criticism was blunt. Questions oscillated around a supposed magic formula that could and would somehow fast track average players to elite levels, which did not come as a surprise. What did come as a surprise was the criticism of people who only viewed the theory and concept robotically. It soon became apparent these individuals struggled to conceptualize the approach, as noted by these two pieces of feedback received from the article.

Interpretation 1: *"10,000 touches a day: if you touch the ball without rest or break every 5 seconds, that is 12 touches per minute which equals 720 touches an hour. So, 10,000 touches only takes 13.88 hours without interruption per day.*

This nonsense is so ludicrous it does not need any careful thought.

I ask this only because I'm curious (really, perhaps pathetically), what qualifies as a touch? The article references "toe-touches, Cruyff turns, drag-backs, pirouettes, juggles, dribbles, or paired one-touch passing the players rested, rotated to a different station, and began another set targeting a different skill." Wouldn't most of those be 1/2 sec. or less? I won't be doing the math."

Interpretation 2: *"It might take a 1/2 second to do something, but you have to be in a position to do it. That is, count one thousand one, one thousand two, one thousand three, one thousand four, one thousand five; in that count, a player would have needed to do something, a ball touch, a move, 10 times. Never going to happen other than a very few minutes of most normal practices. It cannot be sustained. The article should have said 1,000 touches/moves a day."*

The takeaway taught me a few things about how people view things at face value.

Firstly, people immediately tried to break down the methods using rigid math and counting. Secondly, those immediately discrediting the concept may have limited experience playing or coaching the game at a competitively high level, which could also indicate they did not have a firm grasp on what high-level training standards looked like. The major thing I learned from the feedback was the underlying assumption that players could start out with no playing experience and ability, and by getting thousands of touches a day on the ball, they could bypass all other elements of development. In reality, the theory applies to players who already possess high-levels of skill and are able to immerse themselves in an environment that fosters quality playing opportunities.

Additionally, much of the feedback reminded me how the world of player development and coaching is still an uncertain place. The most aggressive group of disparagers had an obligation to challenge new methods and screamed the loudest. Many demanded instant answers, opting to view technical development in terms of a microwave instead of a crockpot. It soon became apparent that people sternly criticized what they did not understand, which is what people tend to do. A concept pertaining to deep practice and reps-based technical training – with the number 10,000 tagged on it – struck a nerve in many circles of player development.

Admittedly, questions like "So when does one get these 10,000 touches? Over the course of a month or a season?" or, "Are you sure you didn't mean 10,000 touches a year or something?" caught me off guard because, to me, the entire process was a normal, practiced routine. I had the same reply every time, "Yes, I meant 10,000 touches each day."

These criticisms remain valuable and even enlightening as they forced me to do a self-audit and deep dive into the practices and methods I believe in.

The thought of doing 10,000 repetitions of anything is insane to most people, but for players on a more serious development track, the task is all in a day's work. Again, I realized people were getting caught up on the number instead of the act of immersion training. From my personal experience, the work itself was a prerequisite to playing at a high level. The same is true for many players who are not considered phenoms or prodigies. Hard work, consistency, and exposure to various training methods for prolonged periods of time at the right stages of their development are critical. The confusion between what I attempted to detail and the effect it had on others and their perception alarmed me because what was normal for me was completely alien to them.

The hourly accumulation of individual ball work resulting in thousands of supplemental touches is the entry fee, not the end goal. That is, simply participating in deep practice is not an accomplishment, but a prerequisite for skill-acquisition and ball mastery. Another problem was my assertion that this type of training does not necessarily result in players leaping ahead of everyone else on the development path – this was merely a piece of the larger puzzle.

The reward for a highly-motivated and disciplined player is *the process*, which isn't always glamorous or comfortable. Top players understand this challenge. For an individual improvement plan of this nature, which is unquestionably arduous, most players will quit before they see marked progress because consistency over an extended timeframe is arguably the most difficult thing to maintain.

76

CHAPTER 9: PROFICIENCY THROUGH PRAGMATISM

At some point, training develops into a transcendent experience to the point it becomes a lifestyle. Personally, getting game-realistic touches by the thousands, each day, was made possible due to a few lifestyle-based decisions and circumstances.

Long before I stepped foot on a plane to Europe, I spent my days playing pick-up games in the neighborhood after school and trained with an organized team that played league games at the weekend. This meant I was playing in some capacity, seven days a week. Growing up in San Jose, California, in the late eighties and early nineties, in a community with a heavy immigrant presence, finding street soccer games was easy. The difficulty, however, was playing in that environment, as the games were generally fierce and disorganized, and regulated by the older players. Their rules and playing conditions always changed to suit their needs.

At the nearby parks, it was clear Latino players were reticent to let others join. Fights and arguments were simply part of the experience. Beyond all the social histrionics, the game was really a series of one-on-many duels. Players learned if they wanted to be picked to partake in these games, they had to play quicker, use more deception, and be confident on the ball. Those who hid in plain sight were simply ignored or told to wait their turn indefinitely on the sidelines.

One of the better players, Ernesto, was 17-years-old at the time. I was 11 and played with the older kids at every opportunity. Most of the time, I was on whatever team was against Ernesto's and the encounters always had that "next goal wins" vibe, although games lasted long after the street lights drowned the courts in an orange hue. Each weeknight, we were out there, and Ernesto ran the show. He seemed to glide through tackles and think three steps ahead of every scenario. He could just as easily dismantle opponents 1v1 or eviscerate an entire team with a precise pass to a teammate making a run.

After a few games, where I held my own and pulled a few tricks out, it was clear I earned my place on the court. However, I had not earned an ounce of respect being both younger and non-Latino. But it didn't matter to me. I knew I wasn't likely to make a lot of friends playing pick-up games. What I wanted to do was get better and I observed Ernesto and studied the way he played the game. His deft touches and ability to dribble and shoot with either foot was impressive, but what I admired was his attitude. He was tough yet respectful. He shook everyone's hand or high-fived them before and after games.

Away from the pick-up game scene, I still found ways to play. In my free time, of which I had plenty, I kicked the ball against our garage door. Most days, my father woke me up at 5 am to either say goodbye and to make sure I woke up for school, or to inform me he was driving me to school that day.

Generally, what prevented me from falling back asleep was playing on my own in the yard or kicking the ball against the curb out front. I remember him buying me a book by Wiel Coerver and Alfred Galustian. The pages contained simple progression-based workouts in a storyboard layout with photographs of youth players decked out in Adidas kits on the greenest pitches, set against a cloudless bright blue sky. The pictures showed sequences of moves and techniques. I studied these pages often and would pick a few to try out whenever I had time to myself.

I started off simple: juggling and dribbling the ball around the backyard with our family Siberian Husky, Apollo, tagging along. My movements would take me to the front yard where I would kick the ball against the curb by the mailbox, knowing it would bounce back at chest height, allowing me to learn how to take balls out of the air proficiently.

Although not every morning was a beautifully functional impromptu training session, the routine was pivotal for my development as a player. Some mornings, I was tuned-in and able to crank out thousands of repetitions before rushing back inside the house to wash up and get ready for school. Other mornings, playing was difficult. In the beginning, the extra work and exercises were something I did to pass the time alone. But after a few weeks, my control and comfort on the ball increased – and it began to show in pick-up games and with my organized team.

The routine, however, was about to change. One morning, as I was juggling in my driveway, I saw a shadowy figure down the street running towards me with an odd gait. As the figure got closer, I realized it was a teenager dribbling a ball. It was Ernesto. He stopped for a brief moment, put his foot on the ball, removed his hood from around his head, and looked at me. After a second, he smirked, popped the ball up in the air, and cushioned a pass to me that I received out of the air. I bumped a lofted pass back to him.

For the next few minutes, we mimicked juggles and passes back to one another in uncomfortable silence. If he took three juggles before passing, I followed suit.

Finally, he broke the silence.

"It's important to practice every day," he said.

"I play out here every day!" I beamed back as a reply.

"Good. But you should do more than kick the ball against the house."

"What do you mean?" I asked, as I fumbled a pass back to him. He was challenging my touch and increasing the complexity of the juggles, and putting more pace on his passes while we spoke.

In one smooth movement, Ernesto took the ball out of the air by cushioning it off his chest, then his thigh, and finally with the ball at his feet, he darted towards me at pace, stopping right in front of me.

"Go running with the ball. Learn to connect it to your foot. Run on the pavement with it, and you'll get faster and smarter."

With that, he tussled my hair and said, "See you around," and he took off on his run with the ball attached to his foot.

The next morning, I woke up earlier than usual to sneak out and dribble-jog around the neighborhood. I searched for Ernesto, hoping to find him so he could see me following in his footsteps in a literal sense, but he was nowhere to be found. It didn't matter; I learned a valuable lesson, which was to add another element of organic training to break the rigidity of foundational movements I was accustomed to performing.

The Practical Chunking Method

Top players often work for prolonged periods of time on specific skills and techniques. To best accomplish this, tasks are segmented into manageable chunks of repetitions. For example, a specific passing technique with either foot will usually involve movement to receive the ball, executing the control and manipulation to prepare to pass the ball, then finally the pass itself. An easier example might simply be juggling the ball for 100 repetitions, followed by 100 passes with a partner or against a wall, followed by another 100 touches on the dribble. High-level players can easily train themselves to reach a level where getting 300 functional touches on the ball is possible in a matter of minutes.

In my experience, players will spend hours each day finding new ways to amass thousands of touches on the ball as quickly, explosively, and – ultimately – as cleanly as possible if they have the right motivation. This requires a strong sense of discipline and a repeatable routine. As with any pursuit, this element of training is borderline obsessive. This is especially true with cultures that have both a playing culture with pick-up games as a cornerstone of their soccer development and with a training culture with organized teams and leagues.

As monotonous and challenging as this route to mastery may seem, it should be noted that players should still have fun. The difference between players on a more serious development path to those who are more casual, is the serious player *has* fun playing, whereas the casual one plays *for* fun. The intrinsic motivations and aspirations of serious players tend to look beyond the superficial aspects of the game by relying on the specific psychosocial domains detailed in Chapter 6.

In serious playing environments, coaches expect players to dedicate extra time and focus to training their specific needs. Historically, a big problem, at least in the United States, is that competitive coaches do not place enough value on the technical and tactical aspects of the game. Instead, the focus at younger ages extends to non-sport-specific strength and conditioning and running protocols. The leads to a version of soccer that relies heavily on hard work and athleticism over technical and tactical superiority. The development approach is misaligned with producing technically and tactically proficient and confident players.

Something like the 10,000 touches a day concept seems borderline obsessive and excessive, and for many, it certainly is overboard. However, the real value is in understanding the approach. Considering that youth soccer, at its core, tends to default to a results-based business and experience, it is not up to coaches to provide every player with all the supplemental training and extra hours to address their specific needs. This is why training and the route to mastery have to transcend traditional methods.

Players undertaking a developmental route involving thousands of game-realistic scenarios and supplemental repetitions a day have made a crucial *decision* to embark on a journey towards advanced areas of the game. On this journey, the rewards and the consequences are steeper than the route taken by most players.

Supplemental training is only a chunk of a larger body of work. Players still need competitive training environments that are both unorganized and organized to test themselves against other players. They must still receive good coaching and meaningful game competition. Additionally, comprehensive physiological, psychological, and tactical qualities are needed to become a professional soccer player.[20]

Prioritizing Development

With respect to applying a method involving the accumulation of thousands of touches on the ball, over time, a baseline level of usable skill must be present for a player to make any marked improvement. Another prerequisite for young soccer players to progress is that they possess a certain level of technical skills.[21]

Logically, the sooner a player can find enjoyment in their immersion in a variety of sports, the better their skillsets and athletic ability can develop. At the youngest levels, it benefits the players to lessen the importance of winning. Tabulating wins and losses as the sole basis for 'development' before 12 years of age can be detrimental to the support systems a player needs. Winning is still important, but it can't be the only important aspect that a player assigns to the game.

Furthermore, there are ways for coaches to still teach the value of victory to players. Even though the objective of the game is to win, it should not come at the expense of learning how to play the game. For example, in Spain and the Netherlands, it's common for youth leagues to focus on learning over winning. In nations focused on youth development over winning, the concept of scoring is viewed differently. For example, stringing consecutive passes together might result in scoring a goal as a learning objective, directly-linked to patterns of play or possession. In these environments, *how* a goal is scored is often more important – and of more use to the team – than merely getting the ball into the back of the net.

Player development combined with a team's game model or playing philosophy should not be sacrificed for winning ugly. When coaches and parents become hell-bent on winning by any means necessary, holistic technical development and proficiency can be devalued. Patience, and

---

[20] Reilly, T., Bangsbo, J., & Franks, A. (2000a). Anthropometric and physiological predispositions for elite soccer. *Journal of Sports Sciences*, 23, 561-572.

[21] Jaric, S., Ugarkovic, D., & Kukolj, M. (2001). Anthropometric, strength, power and flexibility variables in elite male athletes: Basketball, handball, soccer and volleyball players. *Journal of Human Movement Studies*, 40, 453-464.

the focus on fundamental skills, are subject to becoming afterthoughts as effort and time are directed towards results-based strategies.

High-volume technical immersion training is a concept that top young players around the world use to improve on a daily basis. Not weekly, but daily. Soccer development is not the same in every country. Regarding rep-heavy training, four areas matter above all else: realistic application, time invested towards the tasks, quality repetitions, and consistency. The manner in which players amass their touches is up to the player to maximize what their environment provides. For example, players can run for miles with a ball at their feet, touching it every other step. Such a practice, if done correctly, ensures a player is getting plenty of chances to touch the ball in match-realistic ways.

Another reality is that not every player can be elite. Supplemental technical training demands a player's time and it is difficult in a variety of ways – maybe too difficult for most kids. This is why the elite players are elite. These players are different in that they are willing to sacrifice much more – for much longer – to attain or maintain high performance levels in highly-competitive environments. Or these players, circumstantially, are equipped to undertake and maintain such a lifestyle along with its training volume demands. The best players treat the game as a lifestyle, not a chore. Additionally, some of these players come from footballing cultures centered around constantly playing games, on the street, at training, and on their own. Imagining a young player willing to pursue that path, and make the sacrifice – dedicating their time to get extra work in every day – is not farfetched.

To fully appreciate the path the world's top players take, it's important to understand the *type* of soccer they are immersed in long before they become top-level players or even professionals. They play in local or regional leagues, often with intense rivalries. The high stakes pick-up game element is also present, and serves as a parallel outlet to their formal training and playing. At a certain point, they're scouted, scooped up by top academies and their environment changes yet again. In many ways, the cycles of development 'reset' as the stakes and competition rise, filtering out more players.

CHAPTER 10: DELIBERATE CREATIVITY

Player development on the global scale is an inexact science. In fact, it's more lifestyle and environment-based than many realize.

Very few promising players make it to the professional stage, and a fraction of those who "make it" are able to stay there for years as the professional game has a way of determining and often shortening the shelf-life of a player's career.

However, there are commonalities, such as circumstances, lifestyle choices, and habit formation patterns that the best players share. Although they might seem obvious, these similarities are massively influential to their overall development – and are difficult to both master and replicate. We know that when a player experiences high levels of success at very young ages, there is no guarantee or indication that the same player will be successful later on in their journey when playing competitively. Additionally, there is research to reinforce the notion that children benefit from and experience more confidence, enjoyment, and social skills from playing a variety of different sports that involve a ball during their upbringings.

In an August 2015 presentation by Dr. Daniel Memmert, at the German Sport University in Cologne, the sports scientist spoke of a concept he and other leading researchers in Germany have developed called the Ballschule Heidelberg ("Ball School" Heidelberg). Developed by Professor Klaus Roth of the institute, the program aimed to provide a holistic method of play using a ball, in any setting, for fun. Children do not become specialists at young ages in one particular discipline, but rather develop into "all-rounders" in many sports based on the way they play with a ball.

For context relating to the Ball School Heidelberg, it is helpful to dig into its inception. By 2004, Heidelberg University's Institute of Sport and Sport Science, which controlled the program, sought to explore innovative sports programs for children to essentially "learn how to play." Coincidentally, the Ball School was in full operation as a pilot program when Germany was well into its revamp of the federation, and working towards the systematic reworking of German soccer at every level after a dreadful performance at Euro 2000. At the time, the German Football Association (DFB) explored different models of learning to help produce better domestic talent, starting from the grassroots levels.

The program initially accommodated more than 2,000 children between five and eight years of age, but children also started a specific curriculum based around play and practice at the kindergarten level. By taking a *general to specific* approach in the motor development and skill levels of the children, the Ball School allowed youngsters to gain experiences in a *variety* of different sports to increase social interaction and learning capacity. Indeed, they could do so in any setting in which they played, whether it was a backyard, street, court, or at the park… without the need for a coach.

Regarding the curriculum, children learned what is called the "ABC of learning to play." For kindergartners in the Mini-ball School, Basic Motor Skills (A) such as kicking, throwing, catching, bouncing, dribbling, hitting, and stopping were taught. Basic technical-tactical skills (B) such as determining the path to (or of) the ball, determining the ideal position to play the ball, positioning and on-field orientation, controlling the ball with possession in groups, and recognizing gaps were emphasized. Basic coordination skills (C) relate to the pressures of time, precision/accuracy, complexity, organization, and variability.

At the primary school ages, the ABC of learning to play evolves. Basic tactical skills (A) focus on positioning and orientation, ball possession (individually and collectively), creating superior numbers (individually and collectively), recognition of gaps, and using any means or options for scoring. Next, children learn to strengthen basic coordination skills relating to pressures arising from feeling the ball (technique and body control), time, accuracy, the complexity of the situation, organizational, situational variability, and physical strain and stress. Last is the basic technical skills (C). The technical skills taught are determining a path to (and of) the ball, recognizing patterns of movements of teammates and opponents, determining the ideal position to play the ball within a space, control of the ball in possession, and control of passing the ball to maintain possession.

It is no surprise that the "ABC of learning to play" has a massive transfer to the required skills in soccer at every level. By focusing on these areas, as part of the curriculum – while promoting positive social interaction aspects such as communication and instilling confidence and freedom to operate – children are able to learn and be creative in stable environments with flexible playing conditions.

Dr. Memmert's experience extends to many clubs, but his work with FC Barcelona tops the list of the high-profile sides he has studied, and collaborated with, in world soccer.

The key points from the presentation revolved around a qualitative study on creativity that included a vetted questionnaire administered to 72 top coaches along with a population of professional players who identified characteristics of what (and whom) they considered to be the most and least creative players.

From the answers collected, the results were streamlined and showed that players up to 14 years of age *and considered to be 'creative players'* had accumulated more deliberate play time than non-creative players.

So, what's the difference between deliberate play and deliberate practice?

Deliberate play is intrinsically motivating, designed to maximize fun, and looks to provide immediate gratification in various settings. It often requires minimal equipment, is flexible, and allows participants to experiment with rules, tactics, participant sizes, and ages. Deliberate play can be viewed as playing for enjoyment and entails what many of us took part in as children, such as playing games on the street or staying after school to play soccer with friends.

Alternatively, deliberate practice is the act of performing highly structured activities and drills in practice, such as working on specific technical skills or tactics.

The purpose of deliberate practice is about explicitly developing the athlete's capability to perform tasks with *a purpose behind each decision*. Here, an individual's training approach is toward specific skillsets and objectives. Research indicates that deliberate practice may *not* be as enjoyable for young athletes compared to deliberate play.[22]

Research has also found that those most likely to embrace deliberate play exhibit training behaviors that align with deliberate practice. Players who logged workouts with a technical coach (or a team) routinely participated in both in-season and off-season workout protocols, and had prolonged involvement (over a span of five or more years training) in structured settings and match play competitions.

In turn, those who played for enjoyment and in a variety of settings were also the players who understood that deliberate practice was a cornerstone of their development. The players who took the best from both viewpoints were the most creative.

---

[22] Côté, J. & Vierimaa, M. (2014). The developmental model of sport participation: 15 years after its first conceptualization. *Science & Sports*, 29, S63-S69.

The idea that creative players accumulate more deliberate play in a variety of sports over a prolonged span of time has been confirmed in studies. Indeed, one such study suggested that national team players participated *in other sport(s)* for longer lengths of time, compared to non-national team players, up until the age of about 15. Researchers conducted interviews with 52 soccer players who were members of Bundesliga teams, plus 50 amateur players who were in the fourth to sixth tier German leagues, to better understand their training histories and non-soccer sports participation during their upbringings.

The study looked to examine the different ages at which these athletes first played soccer, organized and non-organized, and what other sports they played besides soccer, and at what age they stopped in favor of dedicating their efforts to full-time soccer. Additionally, the research team explored the different types of training they took part in, such as strength and conditioning, skill-based and technical drills, and actual gameplay.

The findings indicated that the professionals playing in the Bundesliga – those reaching the pinnacle of German soccer – averaged around 4,300 hours of intense practice before making their way to the top level of the game. Those who progressed as far as the German national team averaged 4,500 hours before the age of 13. The professional players played more non-organized soccer along with more non-soccer sports in general. Perhaps the most interesting finding was that the earlier the players joined select teams and *eliminated* other sports from their lives, the less likely they were to make it to the senior professional team level.[23]

This lack of premature sports specialization is important as exposure to a variety of sports, and competition styles and demands, aids in overall maturity and produces diverse athletic development.

The study also illustrated that even at Under-19 national level, two-thirds of players' training time was dedicated to club training, with the remaining one-third of training time doing sport "in leisure". In other words, there is a certain point where formal, structured, and coached environments provide the main setting for a player to fully maximize their potential. Free play and unstructured environments are critical, but only to the point where individual development is directly tied to team-

---

[23] Hornig, M., Aust, F., & Güllich, A. (2016). Practice and play in the development of German top-level professional football players. *European Journal of Sport Science*, 16, 96 – 105.

based performance. No matter how good a player does on his or her own, they must be able to operate effectively in a team setting.

Further analysis of the study revealed that deliberate practice accounted for approximately 25% of the holistic training a player accumulated on the way to achieving levels of performance considered "world-class". Deliberate practice, in this context, refers to a special type of practice that is both purposeful and systematic. While regular practice might include mindless repetitions, deliberate practice requires focused attention and is conducted with the specific goal of improving the performance of a specific task, such as position-specific exercises at high-volume and frequency. These findings may lessen the influence that Anders Ericsson (the godfather of deliberate practice) garnered with the 10,000-hour theory, and much of the initial theorizing has been dismissed as parts of his original theory have been refuted. Current research suggests deliberate play is more beneficial to the overall enjoyment of playing than deliberate practice.

It is important not to confuse destiny with opportunity in this context.

Genes and natural attributes provide opportunities, but they do not determine one's destiny. Think of it as a game of cards. You have a better chance of winning if you are dealt a better hand, but you also need to play the hand well to win. This is a crucial part of understanding and exploring development in this context. Regardless of where a player decides to apply themselves, deliberate practice can help maximize potential — no matter what cards get dealt. Deliberate practice turns potential into reality.

So, what does this mean in soccer?

It means that players need to engage in both deliberate play and deliberate practice. On the surface, the logic suggests that players willingly engaging in an activity out of pure enjoyment must also identify with a primary purpose for playing that is centered on maximizing their ability. Players who can leverage both deliberate play and deliberate practice are much more likely to go farther than those who only engage in one or the other. The balance must be right for each player, though.

The individuals subjecting themselves to rote training in an attempt to master individual tasks and skills may burn out and struggle to enjoy the activity. After all, what's the point of training if you don't enjoy playing?!? On the other hand, those who simply play without focusing on highly-structured skill domains, may enjoy the game, but their skillset will plateau as they are not improving specific areas of their game that are required to progress. Additionally, these players are not keeping pace with their competitive talent pools.

However, deliberate practice *does not* necessarily mean that an individual can sculpt themselves into anything with enough work and effort. While people possess a remarkable ability to develop their skills and abilities, there are genetic and circumstantial limits to how far any individual can go. And although genetics greatly influence performance, they do not *determine* performance.

One of the best illustrations of a player's willingness to play (or, to get better) while applying extra training to meaningful competition is Frank Lampard. Early in a player's development, the desire to eagerly engage in better playing methods (training, games, creative alternatives that apply to their evolution as a player, etc.) with more frequency, over time, results in the type of habit-formation we see in established professionals.

In an interview with *The Telegraph*, Harry Redknapp described the scene of privileged youngsters arriving at West Ham United's Chadwell Heath training ground in the mid-1990s. Most of the youngsters played and applied themselves until it was time to go home. But one player, in particular, stayed behind for hours. Alone.

"I'd be sitting in my office at West Ham, four in the afternoon, it would be getting dark, raining and I'd see somebody two hundred yards away," Redknapp recalled. "At first I thought someone had climbed the fence."

It became clear to Redknapp that the shadowy figure training and working in solitude was not a local trespasser. It was someone more familiar to Redknapp – his own nephew, Frank Lampard.

"It was him, always him. From 15, 16 [years of age], every time I looked out there, he'd be out there training. He'd be doing doggies, sprints, dribbling the ball in and out of cones. And shooting. Every single day. Without fail. He was at it from an early age. Still is. He trains harder than anyone I've ever seen by a million miles. He's got a fantastic drive and determination. Far more than anyone else I've ever met in football, actually than anyone I've ever come across."

Much of this is well-known and, yet, it's still profound. Let's review what Frank Lampard was actually doing while he was training alone. He was separating the pieces of the game he needed to improve on and working on them repeatedly until those skills became part of his holistic game. In other words, he was using supplemental training – running soccer-specific sprints, dribbling at game speed, shooting while moving – every day on a consistent basis. His performance was maximized by the quality and frequency of his input (the extra training) over time.

The Need for Multiple Disciplines

So, how do supplemental activities – that are seemingly unrelated to a primary sport – help development? It's no secret that high-level athletes have to leverage a variety of competencies such as speed and strength, endurance and flexibility, intelligence and creativity, and intensity and composure, amongst others. A great place to start this connection is exploring a hidden performance strategy accomplished in jiu-jitsu, Wing Chun, and other martial arts. Students of these martial arts are no strangers to adopting a supplemental sport to enhance the performance of their primary sport.

For the most dedicated students of martial arts like jiu-jitsu, the supplemental training is not centered on weight lifting to bulk up – as strength is important but not nearly as important as technique and body control. So, practitioners use yoga as a part of the discipline because it aids with breathing and controlling inhalations and exhalations to regulate the body and mind. Yoga also improves flexibility to help strengthen the joints, mind-muscle connection, and core strength. Yoga demands focus through meditation – a skill necessary for a competitor to maintain composure and control of their emotions when they are locked in rolling exercises or an actual confrontation that goes to the ground.

An athlete's background also plays a significant role in how they adopt or use supplemental training to improve in a primary sport. In any sport, athletes come from a variety of general backgrounds. In general terms, there are those of relative affluence and those who are not – the haves and the have nots. Obviously, the mindset of athletes will differ as their lives are dramatically different. However, when it comes to development, there may be hidden advantages for each subset of athlete.

For the more affluent athlete, he or she will likely have the means and access points to amenities and specialized training personnel and environments that allow them to streamline their training more. This aids in creating players who understand the different areas of their development that need focus, and provides multiple platforms for them to address the varied needs of their game.

On the other hand, throughout the history of the game, a large percentage of players arise from environments that have a wide array of circumstantial disadvantages. These could range from war, poverty and economic disparity, political oppression, lack of access to scouting networks, lack of familial, social, and sporting support systems, and more. Regardless of what type of circumstance a player is a part of, the indelible fact remains that the number of hours they must invest in their own progress likely exceeds Ericsson's 10,000-hour theory in relation to deliberate play and deliberate practice. Many of the hours a player must invest in their game, throughout their journey, comes in the form of 'unlogged' time – hours spent in activities other than soccer that indirectly contribute to holistic soccer development.

In many parts of the world, a player may have to run or cycle to and from training, day after day, for years as a necessity. In so doing, that player is building up the mental and physical capabilities that strengthen their minds and bodies and solidify their commitment to their craft. Whilst most players are fortunate enough to avoid the demanding routines that hinder opportunities to play, in Mohammad Salah's case, traveling in excess of 100 miles round trip each day by bus or van to play for his club was normal, and it was a sacrifice he had to make in order to advance as a player.

In Costa Rica, I regularly saw players in San José turn a leisurely jog into a brisk tempo run from places like Barrio Tovar to Paso Ancho, or Avenida 12 to Alajuelita or Vista Clara, each of them covering miles with a ball at their feet or in their backpack. This aspect of a player's journey is often romanticized because so few people on the outside – looking in – can relate; or it's a thematically endearing tale of perseverance. But both players of hardship and of affluence must still play the game well, log the hours others are unwilling to log, and prove themselves (while staying committed) for *years* to maximize their potential.

Much like fitness work, the reality of building technical ability requires a highly-structured methodology that must be applied correctly. Factors such as intensity, prolonged duration and repetition over time, and consistency can aid skill acquisition. But where it really matters is in *meaningful competition*. The more soccer-specific tasks, such as running with a ball, that get performed outside of traditional training and games – and which develop into supplemental methods – the better for placing dedicated players at a distinct advantage. In essence, a dose of desperation can actually enhance player development.

Deliberate practice in any discipline requires dedication. But care is needed. In addition to being physically taxing and time-consuming, approaching supplemental training with recklessness and misguided coaching can drive a player into regression. Negative practice habits form in the same way that positive habits do – through repetition and reinforcement. Since writing my article on the 10,000-touches a day concept, I have seen the method approached entirely incorrectly. The results are disastrous. The convoluted implementation of coaches adopting and marketing the concept haphazardly and opting to favor reckless speed and robotic movements – over match-realistic movements and fluid technique – is disheartening. If players train like robots, they will play like robots.

All of this comes down to the role of *rewards* in development and coaching instructions. At the core of most misguided training programs, the focus becomes the command, not the execution of the skill. Creating robotic players is easy as most players want to please their coaches and are willing to conform to their instructions. But, players need to see the logic in the tasks set before them. When that happens, players can find ways to take it upon themselves to train their own deficiencies through supplemental work.

A Happy Medium

A common question I receive is, "As a coach what should we use… deliberate play or deliberate practice with players?" This is a tricky question and not one that I can answer for another coach. What I do know is that when Dr. Jean Côté, a Professor and Tenured Director at the School of Kinesiology and Health Studies, at Queen's University in Canada, and his colleagues conducted their research on the developmental models of sports participation, they offered guidance on which approach should be used at each of the main stages of youth development.

This model is structured in such a way that it categorizes the timespans of development. In a player's younger years (ages 5-11), which are called the Sampling years, training must usually involve a high amount of deliberate play. This is the age range when children are introduced to concepts of sport such as practice, direct instruction, procedures, rules, and group dynamics of soccer, for example.

During this stage, deliberate play gives children more opportunities to develop key 'fundamental movement skills' as the foundational pillars necessary to develop more focused sports-specific skills at the next stage of their development. Additionally, deliberate play also allows young players to develop better gross motor skills, improve their brain function, enhance their physical coordination, posture and balance, confidence, social skills, emotional control, creativity and imagination, which are all important for future performance.[24]

The next stage is what is known as the Specializing years (ages 12-15). Here, players begin to focus their involvement on one or two sports

---

[24] Balyi, I., Way, R. & Higgs, C. (2013). *Long-term athlete development.* Human Kinetics.

with one being their preferred sport. As they begin to specialize, a player's training tends to move into a 50/50 split between deliberate play and practice. This is the stage where players must intently work on skill development for future performance such as general tactics in different formations, sports-specific and position-specific skills, plus increased physical skills such as a greater emphasis on developing fitness and strength levels. All of this is necessary to develop. However, the aspect of having fun and playing for pure enjoyment through deliberate play is still ever-present and important. This way, a player enjoys playing the game and has a higher chance at remaining within soccer instead of opting to quit or play a different sport.

The final stage for a player in this development model is what is called the Investment years (ages 15-18). This is the stage with the most consequence and pressure. A high level of sporting, emotional, physical, and financial investment has been devoted to playing one sport. An example would be a player in a soccer academy or a high-level club that has a view to playing at a professional or elite level. Here, the training shifts in favor of a higher focus on deliberate practice because – in this stage – players must spend more time and effort developing the specific skills for future performance to hopefully compete at a professional or elite level.

The Long Term Athletic Development Model indicates that this age is when players begin to knowingly 'train to compete' and 'train to win', which reinforces the need for deliberate practice.

But what happens to players that don't make it through these stages or cannot sustain the levels required to advance? Based on this model, when players do not move into the Specializing years and eventually, the Investment years, or they drop out at any point, they move into what Côté and his team call the 'Recreational Years'.

This is perhaps the stage with the highest number of players. Here, individuals are not training to make it as a professional or even at the collegiate level, but simply to play the sport for enjoyment. Côté recommends a high amount of deliberate play in this stage; there is no need to spend large amounts of time improving skills... the main goal is not to win, but to have fun.

CHAPTER 11: THE CAULDRON OF THE CAGE

He is best who is trained in the severest school.

Thucydides

In-between graduate school class sessions, each weeknight – underneath the ever-present orange hue of the urban glow nestled in downtown Chicago's Loop – I watched a vacant basketball court come to life. Once the corporate commuters found their way out of the city's downtown district, the streets no longer surged with traffic in every direction, and a new pack of people appeared. City life at night is an odd thing; people still roam the arteries of the city, some with intent; others simply meander beneath the skyscrapers. Joggers and cyclists enjoyed the freedom the streets afforded once the sun had gone down, and the taxi drivers looked for customers with more fervor.

Like all major cities, Chicago doesn't sleep and, on that basketball court, I began to watch something I'd seen in my childhood and on my visits to Europe – street games.

Each night, the first players to show up immediately tossed their bags to the ground and began a casual shooting regimen. Initially, what caught my eye wasn't seeing if the shots went in or not, it was the pattern in which the shots took place. Starting near the free-throw line, a continuous calibration took place with each subsequent shot attempt. If there were multiple players to one ball, it was simply a "make it, keep shooting" scenario. When the small group felt satisfied with extending the range and complexity of the routine, they adjusted.

What started out as a relaxed shooting ritual turned into a well-rehearsed tuning period for the players arriving before the others showed up. Before long, more players arrived, and a half-court game would start. As more players made their way to the court, a full-court game broke out. The astonishing part was that when the games ended, a few players remained to shoot and dribble against their shadows in what seemed like hundreds of game-realistic scenarios. By the time I made my way to the nearby station for the train after class, the court lights would flicker off, and yet I could still see the shadowy silhouette of the basketball hoop hanging in against the dim lights of the urban backdrop.

As fun as those basketball games looked, it was clear these players took it seriously. Every shot had a purpose, and every play had a game-realistic application. Shouting was normal, and hard fouls went uncalled. Basketball, at least in the U.S., is very much like soccer in other countries in that it's accessible in most urban areas. Additionally, many cities have competitive leagues that function as filtration systems for talented players who must often find their way in and out of the street ball scene. Such an environment tests players and their skillsets in unique ways. It also creates a special type of player – one who must be tough and resilient, yet creative and tactically flexible depending on the competition and what the environment presents.

On the global soccer scene, reality is ruthless. The vast majority of players aspiring to play professionally will not make it. Additionally, it is no secret that progress and developing a better and more robust talent pool (or generation) requires deep immersion, playing in a myriad of environments. Just as many of the best basketball players hail from the streets, many of the world's best footballers honed their craft on the courts and streets, too. One notable example is Robin van Persie who sharpened this aspect of his trade on the streets of Rotterdam.

A Sculptor's Son with a Street Football Education

In the Netherlands, street football is part of the sporting culture, and young players from the age of five to 17 are firmly immersed in street football as well as club football. Robin van Persie developed in Kralingen, a suburb of Rotterdam. From a young age, he played with older players from a variety of different ethnic and socioeconomic backgrounds in a cage surrounded by wire fencing and mesh.

Most of the players were Moroccan, two of whom went on to play professionally. Saïd Boutahar played for Real Zaragoza and Al Wakrah, and Mounir Hamdaoui played for AZ Alkmaar and Ajax, amongst other clubs. Both, like van Persie, played for local Rotterdam club SBV Excelsior although van Persie played youth football at the club before debuting for Feyenoord.

However, long before his illustrious professional career, the foundation of Robin van Persie's development started with his time playing street football in Rotterdam. He was part of the vibrant culture that celebrated freedom, creativity, bold skill, and a fixation on the ultimate street football move: the *panna* (a nutmeg). In that world, van Persie mastered his technique and boldness on the ball. As the son of a sculptor and an artist, the football that van Persie played as a youngster was artful and aesthetic.

Growing up, van Persie played in district tournaments where neighborhoods played against one another on makeshift small-sided concrete pitches in five-a-side matches. To stay on the pitch, the winning team had to score two goals within five yards of the goal. The losing team was out. Teams were selected on-the-spot, so the sides were always different – forcing players to learn how to cooperate and adjust their game as both individuals and as a collective. One summer day, van Persie's teams won 40 games.

One account of Robin van Persie's upbringing details his love affair with the football, as told by Dutch journalist and writer, Leo Verheul:

> "I saw him frequently on the street, always with a ball, always. Going to school, he would have the ball at his feet, making feints against every lamppost on his way. Going to the shop for his father, he would keep the ball up, preventing it from touching the ground. But he didn't stop when he entered the store. With the ball in the air, he grabbed what his father had ordered, paid and went off, the ball still dancing. The owner of the shop was an extremely friendly Pakistani man, who smiled an almost offensive amount. He liked Robin but sometimes he lost his smile. Robin had a habit of dribbling with the ball through the store making *pannas* on customers. Some people hated that, were scared or irritated, but the kid just couldn't resist. Or, balancing the ball in the air, he would kick it gently with his heel against the large window of some bar, shop or office, take it smoothly and walk on. Behind him, you saw the heads of surprised people asking themselves what the noise had been."

van Persie, himself, described his relationship with the ball to Verheul in a 2014 article in *The Guardian*.

> "Football has always been my great love. I slept with a ball – really! Even when I started going out with Bouchra – ouha! She must have thought, 'What's this...?' When I was five, I joined a club, Excelsior, the club of Kralingen, in the first division. I was always training. On a free afternoon, I did

individual work with Aad Putters, my youth trainer. Not with the idea of growing to be a star, but for fun. I didn't want to do anything else. When friends wanted to go to the center of town, they took a bus or tram. I took the ball and went running after them. School was hell because I had to put the ball on the ground. Outside I was free, playing the ball."

In many ways, Robin van Persie's life was consumed by his obsession to play. School and homework were of little interest to him, and his father soon learned his son's energy was best spent playing football in the cages and courts around Rotterdam. By the time he turned 13, van Persie had joined Feyenoord, where he could train in a professional setting with top coaches and players. In this environment, his skill and creativity were given structure.

In 2005, a 21-year-old van Persie – pushing to make it on the team-sheet at Arsenal – reflected on his days playing street football in an interview with *The Independent*.

"My left foot is because of the street," said the 21-year-old. "In the beginning, it was poor. When I was eight, nine, 10, it was nothing. I didn't realise that it was good for me. But I like the game, so I shot and shot and shot. Goal after goal."

Beyond the skills and tricks, street football teaches players harsh lessons that require mental strength. In the same interview, van Persie said, "There were lots of better players than me. They were fantastic with the ball, with fantastic tricks. I know a lot of guys who were brilliant but not strong enough in the mind. When I go back to Holland, they say, 'I should have taken my chance. You took it, and I'm proud of you.' And I say, 'You were ten times better than me, but you messed up.' If you want to make it in football, you have to take your chances and be patient."

Closed systems close the doors of opportunity

Optimal player development requires a combination of free, unstructured play that test a player's resolve and skill, plus improved creativity through professional-track, organized playing environments, and high-level coaching guidance.

Ideally, players and teams can exist in an *open*, meritocratic system that rewards both good business moves off the field, and club performance on the field.

In a *closed* system that has no club promotion or relegation, development stalls because there are no solidarity payments to youth clubs who do the bulk of the initial heavy lifting in developing players. There is no reward to those clubs if their best players are merely siphoned off without payment, or percentages of the transfer fees reinvested into the club.

The best players in a system cannot be considered truly world-class talents until they are literally and figuratively competing on an equal playing field. In the United States, for example, when Major League Soccer and the other leagues of the American soccer pyramid under the direction of the Federation (USSF) decide to place importance on rewarding development by way of an open system, the talent base will increase. The reason being that in an open system, teams have to produce or find talented players to avoid relegation, and every team wants to gain promotion.

Smaller clubs have opportunities to advance through the tiers of the pyramid. Communities begin to fashion and align themselves with local clubs to help solidify the marketability, the business model and practices, and actual product; in an open system, communities tend to benefit from the sporting attractions around them. Scouting is an industry that forces clubs to scour the networks available to them to find players that fit their needs and profile types. The trick is recognizing the correlation of building a strong soccer-centric community while developing talented players that will perform and help the club win, or (and more likely) be sold in the open market. Clubs receiving solidarity payments (as mandated by FIFA) can use the funds accordingly.

In a truly global competition pool, poor development practices are exposed and punished. Systems that build from the bottom-up are better positioned to succeed at the top level. This makes sense because the talent pool is not only more robust, but the quality of players existing and emerging from these systems must compete with others within the system to gain promotion and stave off relegation. Similar principles apply to capitalist ideals.

In the United States, there is still no cohesive or truly recognized scouting network immersing itself in the inner cities, local parks, massive youth tournaments, and ethnic leagues for talent. There is no incentive as players are funneled to college soccer, priced out through pay-to-play, and subjected to limited trials that haphazardly assess players who have never played a nine-month season (college is, at most, a three or four-month-long season).

Additionally, the lack of development and the model of importing big-name stars – attacking midfielders and strikers well beyond their prime – on big dollars to compete against inferior talent provides little in terms of improving the overall quality of a league. Importing talent well beyond their "sell-by dates" sells tickets, replica kits, attracts casual fans, and secures corporate sponsorships, sure – all of which play a role in growing the game – but much of this has been done at the cost of marginalizing domestic players and imposing too low a ceiling on player development.

What the street game teaches a player

So what does all of this have to do with the street game? Soccer, like all sports, requires a cultural connection to thrive. Soccer is also a game that hinges upon access to playing environments and resources. In the absence of those environments and resources, individuals must then become resourceful to get opportunities to play regularly. Playing in the streets, empty parking lots, local parks – these are requirements for a system to foster a player like Frank Lampard, who at a young age saw the path from the bottom to the top and who was willing to spend thousands of hours training on his own to validate the role that supplemental training plays. Juxtapose that scenario with one where players are priced out, funneled to a closed league system, and where youth coaches and amateur clubs aren't incentivized to produce talent on a par with the rest of the world.

Change occurs when the cause of a problem, not just the need for a cure, is treated. At the youth levels, where players are taught to win at all costs, the first victim is learning the fundamentals. The purpose of organized youth soccer should not be wholly results-driven. Better technical and tactical awareness, combined with soccer-specific fitness, yields better learning and consistently positive performances. It's no secret that when youth soccer is fueled by money, entitlement comes to the fore. Players and parents become customers, which is a disaster for coaches whose jobs hinge upon the revenue streams of these "customers". Again, true development takes a backseat to winning at all costs and appeasement.

In pay-to-play models, those from lower socioeconomic backgrounds can rarely afford to pay the exorbitant fees the top academies and clubs charge. The pay-to-play model detrimentally dilutes the sport's development. When a youth club aims to 'make money' over developing talent due to the system it exists in, the result is recycled mediocrity.

Simply put, there is a limited street soccer culture that is fostered, cultivated, covered, or encouraged in the United States or Canada. That version of the game is ever-present in Europe, Africa, Asia, and South America and, yet, it only exists in tiny pockets in the United States and Canada.

Players like Neymar, Frank Lampard, Alexis Sanchez, Pelé, Maradona, and an endless list of world stars were street players. They had an organic culture to support the game they played. These types of players take their experiences and attributes from the informal and supplemental, and develop individualized training methods that revolve around getting thousands of supplemental touches a day. Needless to say, this type of training is still an anomaly for many players. Training methods that place an onus on the individual in a system lacking a truly organic process are often overlooked because success has been diverted away from development and equated with money spent. Supplemental training isn't discouraged; however, it's not encouraged to the point where scores of players are training like their counterparts around the world, or in a sport like basketball where pick-up games have a cultural and fundamental presence.

The future, however, is quite bright, and players are beginning to utilize a multitude of resources to improve themselves as players and athletes; resources that may not have been readily available to previous generations. The world's game is more connected, too, through the global reach of the Internet and improved television coverage of the top leagues. Another promising factor – one that could make all the difference – is coaching education. For the first time, an entire generation of players who played a modern variant of the game, and received good instruction themselves, are graduating to the coaching ranks. Additionally, coaches that have more access to better methods tend to become eager learners and are more willing to adopt best practices from around the world.

The role of supplemental practice has to be connected with viable success on a global, not a local, scale. I contend that it is not enough to show a soccer player that extra training will grant them opportunities at the next level. The connection must be made whereby players are willing to adopt a sense of desperation similar to what players around the world live with to become elite. Establishing that connection shifts the paradigm away from the recreational toward the more serious track, which helps both the lower levels and top levels of the game.

Consider this. In the United States, a large percentage of soccer players come from suburban environments and don't necessarily have a built-in drive to maximize the resources they may (or may not) know are at their disposal; resources such as access to online training platforms, progressive coaches who understand the need for training methods that are more applicable to the modern game, and training centers such as gyms, indoor facilities, and state-of-the-art training complexes that continue to pop-up across the country. American players need to utilize the nation's multicultural diversity; it is wholly possible to play in a multitude of representative environments, whether that be in cages and courts, on the streets, or in futsal leagues – to name a few – within the contiguous U.S. if the game becomes more accessible.

By its very nature, historical growth, and expanding popularity, soccer is inherently a multicultural sport that has been diluted and sanitized for largely suburban populations. For the sport to truly permeate a country's cultural fabric, it must not only be present but celebrated across as many socioeconomic levels and environments as possible. Nations producing talented generations of players, capable of playing in the world's top leagues, have access points to the game at the granular level – often starting with the street game from a very young age.

In researching this topic, I once again spoke with Terry Michler (an advocate for street soccer and futsal in his coaching methods) about the impact of street soccer and even futsal on improving foot skills, technical ability, confidence on the ball, and overall player development.

"Street soccer was the building block for most professional soccer players back in the days before automobile traffic. Street soccer today has become small-sided games (four, five, or more, a side) and futsal. The value of street soccer and small-sided games (SSG) and futsal is that you are reproducing the game in a smaller dimension, but still have all the elements present that represent the real game of 11 v 11. Every soccer action is performed and repeated many, many times.

"Players become more familiar with the recurring situations and can more easily adapt, recognize and respond to them. Immediate feedback of success or failure is present, and adjustments can be made quickly to any failed attempts. The increased number of touches, 1v1 duels, scoring opportunities, defending, and transitions that occur are endless. In 11v11 soccer, a player only has a very limited number of contacts with the ball and the game in general. With the increased size of the playing area and the increased number of players, it just makes the individual's involvement less frequent.

"Street soccer, SSG, and futsal (the modern version of street soccer) allow players to make more decisions, be in more contact with the ball, work with teammates and against opponents, and have fun doing it, while improving themselves.

"One more point about street soccer – the players controlled the game, made up and enforced the rules, no adults overseeing it, and the game was played with whoever was available at the time – boys, girls, mixed ages – it did not matter. Surfaces were not pristine – rough cobblestone streets, patchy dirt fields, certainly not the plush carpet turf fields of today.

"The players had a much bigger challenge managing the ball because of the variety of poor surfaces they played on. Thus came the importance of the relationship they developed with the ball. The odd bounce was always going to happen and you had to be ready for it. Dennis Bergkamp, when growing up, would kick a ball off a wall to see all the different ways it would come back to him, and he would then have to control it. He would do this by himself for hours on end. It worked for him and he became one of the technically best players of his time."

Concrete Football

The documentary *Ballon sur Bitume* (Concrete Football), released in 2016, celebrates street football in France. The film provides a great glimpse into the culture that has continued to nurture some of the most celebrated talents in international soccer, while showcasing how community and talent have joined forces on concrete pitches to overcome adversity in urban arenas. In addition to having a robust history in the sport, France also celebrates and integrates sport with its diversity as a country.

Manchester City's Riyad Mahrez is one of the voices featured in the film. He explains how the environment helped him develop the skills he is renowned for at the professional level.

"When you're living in the housing estates, you play outside all the time," Mahrez said. "Our parents aren't that strict and so they let us play, and playing all day every day really helps you improve your dribbles and technique. I think that's why the best technical players come from the streets."

In France, street football is part of a wider culture in the housing estates known as *les banlieues*, which are made up of housing units that lie on the outskirts of French cities but which aren't quite considered suburbs. These areas are inhabited by working households, often with single parents, that pay taxes but lack the public services, education, transportation, employment opportunities, and access to other amenities that support the city proper. *Les banlieues* are, in some ways, their own cities with their own rules and politics that extend into sport as a societal function.

Over the last 40 years, *les banlieues* have gained a reputation for social problems with critics identifying high numbers of immigrants, along with people of low socioeconomic backgrounds, being a cause of overall perceived problems; problems such as higher crime rates, acculturation, lower standards of education, issues with housing, a lack of employment opportunities, and differences in social functionality and identity as they relate to societal differences. The documentary *Ballon sur Bitume* takes a different look at these areas and celebrates the stories and pursuits of the young people who call *les banlieues* home.

In an interview with the *Guardian*, co-director Jesse Adang said, "Zinedine Zidane was the first Arab guy from the suburbs in Marseille who was playing at such a high level. He's a hero for people like us. [Hatem] Ben Arfa, too. His story is crazy, he stopped playing for a while and he trained with street football during a period to keep his level up, and now he's at PSG. You can see that people love him for that when he comes out on the pitch."

The documentary supports the popularized principle that footballers whose beginnings in the sport started in the streets are undoubtedly products of environments that toughen them up in the absence of written rules and sensibilities, and which serve to prepare them for the challenges of not only attempting to play at a professional level, but in life itself.

Ballon sur Bitume also provides insights into the psychological drivers that help produce talented players in a ruthless and gritty grooming school of street football. Riyad Mahrez explains, "The ribbing, trash-talk, there's certainly a psychological element to it. Sometimes in the tournaments you can hear them shouting things like 'kill him'. We grew up with that. That's why, when you become pro and you're up against an opponent, you know you have to just make the pass and make the difference."

An Inexact Science

The street soccer environment can challenge aspects of an individual's personality and life off the field in ways that conventional training may not. It forces players to be crafty and independent. It instills a degree of maturity and thriftiness that can't be coached into a player. The street game is about freedom, toughness, and a lifestyle where the game and freedom of expression is the ultimate reward. In this world, a player's pride is at stake and at risk every time they take to the concrete. Social standing in street football can operate as a social currency.

However, what makes a street player great may very well keep them off the pitch in a structured environment. What top players require is a *mixture* of both environments, which may not always be possible. Training the structured and tactically-valued aspects of the game is as much a reps game as getting lots of pick-up games and logging hours playing in that cauldron. Traits like leadership, toughness, self-coaching, teamwork, innate motivation, self-analysis, self-critiquing, and self-regulated fitness regimens can be honed outside of the structured environments, but to what end?

Although the romanticized aspects of street soccer remain pure, free, and vibrant and – in many ways – it operates as a function and extension of life and society for many aspiring players, there's an irony to it as well. The street environment serves as both a haven and home for those with dreams of elevating themselves from their roots to a life playing at the highest achievable level. But, it can hold a player back if they cannot learn the rules or way of life required to make entry into the formal and structured footballing world where players must be coachable, stay out of trouble, not party every night, and play in a team dynamic. As Robin van Persie's and Riyad Mahrez's stories illustrate, there are specific skills, traits, connections, and even circumstances that must align for an individual to leave the street soccer scene for greener pastures.

The reality is what makes a great street player may very well keep them off the pitch in structured environments. Although these games require creativity and afford players more touches on the ball on a faster surface, street soccer revolves around doing imaginative tricks and has followed an evolutionary trajectory centered on small-sided games.

At some point, players have to make the leap from playing on the courts and in the cages to the structured game. It is at this precipice where many players face aspects of the game that challenge them in ways other than their skill on the ball. Their ability to listen, stay disciplined, understand tactics and remain coachable – these are traits that are honed in structured environments where the emphasis is on "We" over "Me" as the game expands into a team dynamic.

The street game in sport teaches many lessons. One of the most valuable, however, is that although it produces the occasional diamond in the rough, that outcome is rare. And if pressure makes diamonds, for every one produced, there are a thousand pieces of crushed coal that get swept away.

CHAPTER 12: THE BELGIAN BLUEPRINT

In Belgium, there's a tired joke that the only "true Belgian" is the king of the country. Woven into Belgium's rich history, there exist long-standing tensions and divisions amongst the population between those who speak French, the Walloons, and the Dutch-speaking Flemish people. From a political standpoint, Brussels defines itself as a multi-cultural symbol of a city that is largely defined as being the capital of Europe… rather than that of Belgium. Sociologically, Belgium's identity as a unified nation often seems unconvincing.

However, there is a unifying aspect that the world has observed on the pitch – Belgian football. As a national team product, the Red Devils have been ranked as high as first in FIFA rankings, and the exports of illustrious (and highly sought-after) Belgian talent continue to flourish in club football through the likes of Eden Hazard, Romelu Lukaku, Kevin De Bruyne, and Thibaut Courtois amongst many others. Over the last decade, Belgian football has bridged many divides by becoming an institution and finishing school for some of the best footballers on the planet. In some respects, football has helped the people of Belgium better define what it means to be Belgian.

Part of what sets Belgium apart is its diversity of players on the national team, which is loaded with well-known superstars playing in some of the best leagues in Europe. And *almost all of them* emerged from the Belgian league system, which has become an export factory of footballing talent. The national squad is a representation of an ever-evolving Belgium with many players from immigrant backgrounds.

It is no secret that the current era of Belgian football was not always held in such high regard. As a footballing nation, Belgium has long been hidden in the shadow of its neighbor, the Netherlands. In fact, the Dutch seemed to always outplay their Low Country neighbors in every aspect of football – from club teams to globally known and revered individuals. To this day, one of football's most iconic images is from the 1982 World Cup, where Diego Maradona is surrounded by six hesitant Belgian players, positioned to be carved through by a lone superstar.

For the Belgian federation, the first of many pivotal moments came in 1998 after Belgium were eliminated in the group stage at the World Cup. Two years later, as the co-host of Euro 2000, Belgium's footballing malaise was on display for the world to see after the Red Devils failed to advance out of the group stage for the second consecutive tournament.

So, what happened? And what can be learned with regards to player development? Are there lessons that can be applied elsewhere? Belgium changed its identity and decided to overhaul its football system. The renaissance needed a spark, and the formation of a new blueprint for the country's football structure needed an architect and a team of visionaries. The first of these figures was Michel Sablon, whom the Belgian federation appointed as its Technical Director in 2002. His task: revamp the entire system.

At the same time, another visionary of Belgian football, Bob Browaeys, played a pivotal role, too. As a former player and coach with experience at every level of Belgium's national youth team set-up, Browaeys played a major role in helping Sablon to develop this new blueprint. From the onset, Browaeys rightly noted that there was no unified vision on youth football at all levels in 1998. His first move was to convene with 30 federation coaches from the Dutch and French-speaking parts of the country to meet and discuss a radical change of approach going forward. As a nation, Belgium had just watched France win two consecutive major tournaments with a diverse team that represented not only France as a country, but also its abundant colonial reach and past. The success of those French teams provided a framework for Belgium, a country with its own rich history and global colonial influence, to usher in a new era of football.

The Melting Pot of Talent

By 2018, the World Cup roster for Belgium included Kevin de Bruyne and Vincent Kompany of Manchester City, Romelu Lukaku and Marouane Fellaini of Manchester United, and Eden Hazard, Michy Batshuayi, and Thibaut Courtois of Chelsea, to name a few. These players, products of Sablon's vision, went abroad for expensive fees that became reinvested in Belgian football. They often joined powerhouse clubs in England, Germany, and Spain and allowed Belgium to display the talent it produces to the eyes of the world.

What is important about this outcome is that, before the 1990s, European countries had strict rules limiting the number of foreign players that could be rostered with a given professional team. This restricted the movement of players within Europe. However, in 1995, a Belgian player named Jean-Marc Bosman successfully argued that these rules violated one of the core principles of the European Union. Namely, freedom of movement between member states. Following the

Bosman Ruling, the transfer of players across Europe skyrocketed, resulting in enormous increases in the transfer fees paid between teams. In turn, Belgian clubs developed and perfected a business model focused on developing young players and then selling them to richer clubs abroad. The small Belgian town and club of Genk, for example, produced Kevin De Bruyne and Thibaut Courtois, and Christian Benteke. The fees for these transfers paid for a major expansion of Genk's facilities and programs.

Christian Benteke represents a common trend in Belgian football's ascension – the colonial impact. Benteke was born in Kinshasa, which was formerly part of Zaïre and is now the Democratic Republic of Congo. His family fled the brutal Mobutu regime and eventually settled in Belgium when Christian Benteke was a young boy.

The Benteke family was part of several generations of migrants from Congo who made Belgium their home. The 2018 Belgium World Cup squad had five players with family ties to the Democratic Republic of Congo, a former Belgian colony notorious for the brutality of its exploitation. Vincent Kompany's family name stems from his lineages' labor in a Belgian company mine. His family fled Congo in 1968 and migrated to Belgium. Romelu Lukaku's father played professionally and represented Zaïre in the 1990s. Michy Batshuayi also has a Congolese background.

One of the most notable stories from World Cup 2018 was the rosters of champions France and Belgium. France, the World Cup champions, had 16 of 23 players in their World Cup squad with African or Caribbean descent. Much like the French team of 1998 and 2000, the colonial presence was evident on the pitch and in the play. Belgium, also, had begun to reap the benefits of first and second-generation immigrants who were part of Sablon's early blueprint. Mousa Dembélé's father is from Mali. Marouane Fellaini's parents are from Morocco. Nacer Chadli's parents also came from Morocco (and Chadli even played on the Moroccan national team before choosing to play for Belgium). Adnan Januzaj could have played for either Kosovo or Albania, based on his parent's backgrounds.

Courts, Cages, Communities

The significance of these players' journeys is clear. These players are highly-regarded and were identified because of Michel Sablon's national training model that included a wider social and civic purpose.

In the late 1980s, at a time when global immigration was on the rise, anthropologist Johan Leman was asked to develop policies for the social "integration" of migrants, to help them assimilate into Belgian society. Leman suggested using football as a mechanism, prompting municipalities to build small, cement soccer pitches in urban neighborhoods. The current Belgian national team is the manifestation of a unique convergence between local neighborhood and urban infrastructure, and the broader national training system.

From an anthropological perspective, Belgium is a diverse country with many nationalities and immigrant pockets contained within siloed communities. By using football as a societal tool, whole communities had a central environment in which to play. To help shift the footballing paradigm, the Belgian FA worked closely with communities, especially those with high populations of immigrants, to build the football courts and cages. The upshot was organic environments in urban centers around the country, which allowed players to get invaluable hours of unstructured, creative, and competitive game-play; on the ball game-play where individuals could hone their techniques like those in the Dutch, French, and German systems.

The aim from the onset was to provide *safe places* for communities to play. Almost immediately, however, Belgium began producing a generation of technically adept, intelligent players at all levels. It seemed that providing the foundational structure for a new national training program required substantial work at the community level. Additionally, the organic game was all about diversity in a multitude of ways, from the type of football played to the type of player who found their way to the courts. The standard of play – which many of the players brought from other countries – intermixed with Belgian street football culture, began to rival that of their illustrious neighbors in the Netherlands.

The result of Michel Sablon's vision was *increased access for more players* throughout Belgium. While this work took place at the community level, the national program that Sablon was architecting would reap the benefits in time. On the surface, the courts and cages built within the communities simply provided a place for youngsters to congregate and play football. From an organizational perspective, they provided a place for coaches to observe players in free environments! What emerged was a collection of observations and behaviors that were immediately applied to the coaching education curriculum.

A New Formation Requires a Different Player

Sablon's revamped model required a different type of player, but it also required a different type of coaching and player development. If the increased speed of play and heightened speed of thought required in an effective 4-3-3 formation was to going to be realistically implemented, the technical ability of the players scouted and identified around the country would require a new standard to which to assess quality.

Coaches and scouts had to understand and observe what the current state of player development entailed, while working towards a more progressive objective. As a result, Sablon and his colleagues compiled what was known as the *Louvain Report*. This report included extensive observation, analysis, and data from all over the country at a variety of professional and amateur clubs, plus grassroots and urban environments, including the courts and cages, and – of course – at the academy levels.

If the primary task required a different type of player to be produced throughout the Belgian football system, there would have to be a cultural change. Grassroots coaches who now had access to revamped and free coaching education courses were trained to focus on observing and understanding their players and their playing nuances, tendencies, and personalities before over-coaching them. The observation period allowed for structured planning to assess what type of players they had, and what their tendencies on and off the ball were during training and match-play. The next step was producing players who were creative yet dominant in one-on-one situations.

For the youngest ages at the grassroots level, removing the emphasis on 'winning' allows youngsters to focus on threading intricate passes, moving off the ball, and playing an open, free-flowing game; players can go from getting four touches every 20 minutes to getting hundreds if not thousands of meaningful touches on the ball each training session. Youngsters in Belgium play *le football de rue* obsessively and, as a result, expedite their technical development due to the increased accumulation of hours playing in fast-paced, small-sided games.

With Michel Sablon firmly in his role as the technical director, the playing philosophy was in place, but it still lacked a grassroots structure. It was up to Sablon to provide further detail on how to remediate a broken youth system. For the next two years, Sablon worked intensively, exploring and identifying the country's shortcomings in the sport from cultural and community levels. Attending numerous Belgian youth competitions and identifying the necessary baseline changes were just the start.

On the business side, the post-Euro 2000 era would prove to be pivotal for Belgium with the money made as co-hosts of a major tournament. One of the major steps in providing the new development structure was

Sablon and the Belgian FA allocating a large sum of the tournament money and sponsor payouts to be entirely invested in youth development. The result was a new national football complex built on the outskirts of Brussels. The federation also focused on coach education and increased the number of people enrolling on the entry-level coaching course tenfold after the federation made the course free of charge.

Next, the consultancy group, Double PASS, was appointed to perform an extensive audit of all the youth systems at club level and make recommendations. The next step was implementing what was identified as the successful methods from the Dutch and French national programs. In his analysis, Sablon tasked researchers to painstakingly deconstruct the domestic game. Sablon got the universities of Leuven, Ghent, Louvain-la-Neuve, and Liege to analyze and detail Belgian football's landscape with an emphasis on youth development.

Michel Sablon believed numbers and objective datasets were the keys to unlocking the country's potential in the sport. He worked with Professor Werner Helsen of KU Leuven's Department of Movement Control and Neuroplasticity to help define the best form of play. Helsen and his students analyzed 1,500 hours of game footage, focusing on the different phases and movement patterns present, such as: short passes, the number of touches of every player on the ball, the build-up method in possession, and the use of the long ball as a pass, panicked clearance, or habit of impatience and frustration.

Helsen believed in Anders Erikson's deep practice theory and stated that the minimum trajectory for an aspiring top player is 10,000 hours. His team looked at multiple game actions with players wearing heart-rate monitors to check the intensity levels of different game forms. Player movement on the pitch was also assessed. At the time of the study, these types of analytics had only been geared towards professional players. They had not yet been configured to the motor and physical movements of youth players.

The 1,500 hours of football footage of young players playing 11-on-11 on full-sized pitches was also to distinguish how often each player (on average) actually touched the ball both in a movement and during an entire game. The findings deduced that each player touched the ball four times in a 20-minute span. In addition to conducting objective and academic football analysis, Sablon held official, mandatory meetings with coaches from all levels to discuss training methodologies, formations, tactics, and remediation plans.

Both audit findings from Double PASS and Sablon's observations and analyses resulted in the finding that was that there was far too much emphasis on winning and not enough on player development. To offset this problem, Sablon eliminated U7 and U8 league tables to shift the focus away from wins and losses. This also highlighted individual player growth. Additionally, there was evidence to support Sablon's theory that 2v2, 5v5, and 8v8 were the best small-sided games to encourage children to practice specific skills such as dribbling and diagonal passing, which are essential to the playing philosophy of the 4-3-3 tactical formation.

The results of the studies weren't absorbed by Belgian football coaches instantly. The iterations of the process required Sablon to deliver more than 100 presentations where he had to validate everything he noted from video evidence and objective datasets and schemas to his audiences of coaches.

The real challenge came when Belgium lost games playing the formation. And yet, another requirement that Sablon had implemented began to pay dividends. Capped players were no longer allowed to go down a level in the national team set-up. For example, a player capped at the senior level could no longer be selected for U21 duty. This streamlined the trajectory of the national players getting senior-level minutes at younger ages and kept a core player pool together for more years. Sablon and the Belgian federation remained resolute, especially at the youth levels. The message remained consistent: development must take precedence over winning, technique must eclipse athleticism.

In an interview with *The Guardian*, Browaeys highlighted the strategy Belgium employed prior to the rebuilding of their system. "You have to know that at the end of the 90s in Belgium, they all played with individual marking, sometimes with a sweeper, it was 4-4-2, it was even 3-5-2. We got a lot of results with our A team, because we played very organized. But it was defensive, a culture of counter-attack."

A significant part of bringing in coaches from the Dutch and French-speaking parts of the countries was to help emulate the ideas and footballing philosophies that were working in the Netherlands and France. In order to tap into the training methods and collective philosophies for the national team programs (and apply those changes), one thing was certain – Belgian football had to fundamentally change in every aspect.

The first step was in understanding what powerhouse clubs, influenced by Dutch and French football, were doing well. By observing and studying what worked well for a club like Ajax, for example, the identity of the *type* of player that would be required began to take shape. The second step was identifying the tactics employed by other countries and clubs. This concept of identifying a game model allowed Sablon and the Belgian FA to overhaul the existing national team program.

Perhaps the most noticeable transformation was the type of player Belgium aimed to produce. In order to accommodate the necessary components present in other national team frameworks (teams deemed more successful), a completely different approach had to take place regarding individual player development plans. All of this required a different type of footballer – the type that Ajax and even Barcelona produced at the individual level. Next, Browaeys, Sablon, and their colleagues proposed that every Belgium youth national team would play a 4-3-3 formation – a decision that would force the federation to begin producing a totally different type of playing style and player profile. Today, the type of player emerging from Belgium has a unique blend of flair, power, intelligence, and creativity – a unique hybrid of immersion in the organic pick-up games on the courts and streets, and the cohesive and organized coaching environments that are now standard.

Browaeys and Sablon believed in the success of the 4-3-3 formation. The downstream effect for implementing that formation, in addition to the training methods and philosophies of successful club and national team programs, would require Belgium to produce 1v1 specialists in every position. Within this game model, these players had to be excellent on the ball with the ability to out-play, out-maneuver, and out-think the opposition without hesitation.

For Belgium to dramatically change their footballing identity, the player archetype would mirror what the French, the Germans, and the Dutch had accomplished. Modern-day players had to be capable of playing in a variety of positions, in different tactical formations, and with an incredibly high level of technical ability and game intelligence. Positional interchange, similar to what the Dutch coaching legend Rinus Michels implemented with his teams, was no longer regarded as a perk to a player's ability, but a requirement of their development. Possession and positional interchange would become a science, and dribbling of all types would resemble a creative art form.

Much like the football on display, the mechanisms that allowed for this revamp remain diverse. Players have a culture of technical excellence and no shortage of environments in which to train and play. Current and future generations have footballing idols to look up to who *grew up in the same cities and neighborhoods* and plied their trade on the same concrete football pitches long before they took the field for clubs like Liverpool, Chelsea, Real Madrid, and many more. For Belgium – moving forward – the trend looks set to continue for future generations.

CHAPTER 13: THE GRITTY GAME

When I was nine years old, my father showed me a clip of Pelé juggling a grapefruit. To be honest, it was an odd clip made for American television in the 1970s when soccer was absolutely seen as an "odd game" played "over there." By the time I saw the clip in 1994, soccer was still considered a foreign game to mainstream American audiences.

I saw the clip in two lights. On the one hand, here was a clip of a man – considered by many to be the world's greatest player – juggling a piece of fruit. Oh, how that would astound American audiences in a minstrel-show-type of way. On the other hand, the display was one of pure skill, ingenuity, and provided a glimpse of the creativity of the game.

For many, watching Pelé do anything with a ball was nothing short of magical. For me, that clip coincided with a scene from the movie *Escape to Victory*, where Cpl. Luis Fernandez (Pelé) juggles a ball on his head while Captain John Colby (Michael Caine) asks, "Where'd you learn to do that?" to which Cpl. Fernandez says, "When I was a boy, in Trinidad, in the streets, with the oranges," while continuing to juggle the ball.

I immediately ran out to the orange tree in the backyard, plucked an orange from a low-hanging branch, and unsuccessfully tried to juggle it like Pelé. To this day, my record of juggling an orange is 12.

What's the point of this story?

At the youth level in the United States, the modern game suffers from the symptoms of an over-scheduled society. This is likely a reality in many countries, but in the United States it's a common issue that affects the growth of the game. For example, each day I follow a routine. Part of this routine involves driving over 35 miles across a state line to St. Louis, Missouri. Along the way, I drive by a total of three public parks (one suburban park and two city parks), each with plenty of perfectly well-kept fields that are lined and outfitted with goals that have nets.

I notice available places to play more due to my upbringing, where I never saw so many perfectly maintained soccer fields outside of a few tournament complexes. Growing up in San Jose in the late 1980s and early 1990s, the nets would be stolen or slashed, the corner flags taken, and the fields would remain unkempt for large stretches. Back to the present day, each of these parks usually has a sign that reads, "Keep off the Field" or "No Play Except on Game Days." Keep off the field? No play except on game days? Even on weekends, or during the summer months, these fields are still devoid of pick-up games, which is odd for St. Louis as it is known for its rich soccer history in the United States.

Every time I visit my parents, who still live in the house I spent my formative years growing up in, I make it a point to go to the very field I spent thousands of hours playing on after school. It, too, sits idle. Nearly 20 years ago, the field was never empty. What was once a bustling park with separate lined fields loaded with players and pick-up games is now a giant barren field. For a time, the grass remained manicured, the goals stayed anchored in place, but what was missing was players honing their craft. In the last two decades, pick-up soccer has seemingly become a lost game. Whether we played "jumpers for goalposts" in the park, or a game my friends and I called "three bar" (a common game in pick-up ice hockey), many of the hours we logged took place outside of structured games and training sessions.

The reality for a majority of young players is that the hours spent in formal, organized practice is simply not enough for maximum technical improvement in soccer. Contrary to what many are led to believe, it is simply not enough to depend solely on these formal sessions. Perhaps what has changed is the value placed on pick-up and street soccer. One could argue that too much infrastructure is in place. Suburban players typically do not partake in pick-up games for a variety of reasons, including a dependence on technology, and parental involvement (or interference) in the form of over-scheduling children in far too many activities. In urban areas, soccer may not have the playing presence or environments that basketball or other sports garner. Additionally, there seems to be a form of cultural apathy where young people see little-to-no value in spending time outside – often preferring to spend their days inside playing computer games.

Johan Cruyff once said, "I trained about four hours a week at Ajax as a boy, but I played four hours on the street every day. Where do you think I learned to play football?" The world over, street soccer and pick-up games teach players to be creative, tough, to work together, and they help build up resilience. Unsupervised and impromptu games provide players with a platform to try out new skills without fear or coaching interference. In many ways, qualities such as leadership emerge along with friendships and rivalries that help develop a player's competitive appetite.

Street soccer, for many, is personal and solidifies a sense of neighborhood pride. Personally, street soccer was part of being a player. Long before we joined structured teams or attended organized practices, we played for the right to come back to play at the courts or at the park *the next time*. Growing up in an environment with a diverse immigrant presence helped me develop more as a person. The player development aspect was secondary, in many ways, as I learned about the game within the game. Admittedly, street soccer was not always a ruthless scrap war. It was also a time to relax and get outside to muck around with friends and, in the process, get thousands of extra repetitions and hours on the ball doing isolated skills and then playing the game.

Empty Fields, Safe Spaces, and Finishing Schools

Today's player is far too over-scheduled with activities that keep them indoors. According to the American Accreditation Health Care Commission, as of 2019, kids spend about three hours a day watching television with additional "screen time" accumulation through tablets, computers, and smartphones. The finding indicates that screen time for children and adolescents can total six to eight hours a day. In addition to the lost time and playing opportunities, kids are more apt to eat junk food; the result is lethargy and extended periods of sedentary time, which has become a lifestyle.

Another contributing factor is the community itself. Parks with signs plastered around the ground prohibiting people from playing on the fields can be problematic. Of course, it's not out of the realm of understanding as facilities managers want to maintain the condition of the fields, nets, and goals. There is also a liability issue that can't be ignored. Signs with "Keep Off" emblazoned in bold lettering send a message that fields have become places where only organized play is allowed.

In many respects, society has evolved in such a way that parents are guilty of (knowingly or unknowingly) competing with one another by using their children as trophies of accomplishment. The result is a type of systemic parental competition where parents over-schedule activities for their kids in an attempt to reinforce the assertion that *their* child is the most talented and well-rounded of the bunch. Of course, there is the factor that many parents want to expose their children to a diverse array of activities and provide opportunities for them that they may have never experienced themselves growing up. However, this over-involvement in an increasing array of extracurricular activities provides a unique conundrum. On the one hand, there are more organized activities and outlets for people than ever before, and individuals should be free to explore and try new things often. On the other hand, in the context of high-level player development, the over-scheduling of activities results in a generation of exhausted, robotic, and unmotivated young people who have grown up being conditioned to need constant prompting.

For players in more urban environments, access to safe places to play can be part of the problem. In a blog post titled "Small Space, Big Impact", former Projects Officer for the U.S. Soccer Foundation, Jim Hannesschlager, addressed the topic of the lack of soccer-dedicated courts and settings. In the short piece, Hannesschlager took feedback from both new and experienced coaches and from players. He wrote, "Facilities are hard to come by… a small, intimate, soccer-specific space is the perfect forum for youth to participate, grow, and fall in love with the game. The U.S. Soccer Foundation's Mini Pitch Initiative is set up to enhance, assist, and grow the beautiful game in places it has traditionally struggled. Whether you want to call it a soccer court, a mini-pitch, futsal, or five-a-side, we are all speaking the same language – creating safe places to play the game in a soccer-specific venue."

While few would disagree with the need for safe, soccer-specific places to play, the likelihood of that ever happening is far-fetched. And if the perfect setting was available, would it create the type of player that can compete on the world stage, or would it lessen the impact of learning the game in a more unpredictable environment? In high-level sports, the onus is ultimately on the individual to find ways to play… even in adverse settings. This remains a complex issue, but building futsal courts and sharing space with basketball courts with the installation of steel goal frames can help provide places to play.

At Brazilian clubs such as Gremio, Fluminese, and Corinthians, and in Argentine clubs Boca Juniors and River Plate, players typically train twice a week until the age of 15. At that point, if they are selected, they join a residency program, which allows these young players to ramp up their training to five days a week for around three hours a day. A similar model is followed at *De Toekomst* (Ajax) and *Varkenoord* (Feyenoord) in the Netherlands.

In top academies, a system exists that steadily increases the dedicated time players spend in controlled environments. By the point a player reaches this level, they've almost certainly logged thousands of hours on the courts, streets, and in the cages fine-tuning their skills. These top youth players must amass thousands of hours and repetitions of supplemental skill work and development away from the structured settings that operate as finishing schools for the elite.

The story of Raheem Sterling's discovery, in the book *The Nowhere Men* by Michael Calvin, details the magnitude that pick-up games had in Sterling's development prior to, and during, his time with Queens Park

Rangers' Centre of Excellence. Along with allowing time for intense, repetitive training, free play allows players to improvise and augment their training. This environment helps players identify *who they are* as individuals away from label-heavy team settings.

Another example of organic development is from the *Tahuichi* academy located in Santa Cruz, Bolivia; a city that suffers from drug-related criminal activity and high crime rates. Many players at the academy use soccer as an outlet, temporary escape, or even as a way out of Santa Cruz. As a result, the *Tahuichi* environment is very different from a conventional academy. Players train on dusty and bumpy pitches daily. Products of the academy are conditioned to overcome the obstacles of playing in such difficult conditions, on subpar surfaces, immersed in an environment devoid of manicured pitches and pressed kits. A large part of the development of these players is rooted in the technical and psycho-social skills honed from playing in diverse and adverse circumstances.

At *Tahuichi*, players emerge from the setting possessing a deft touch paired with a high level of body and ball control from training on uneven surfaces and bumpy fields, so when they play on flat fields with actual grass – their speed of play and technique elevates. The fitness development and connection with preparing their bodies and minds for competition are also unconventional. Instead of running on treadmills or paved sidewalks, players run through streams and up sand dunes (oftentimes with a teammate on their backs) to build strength and maintain their conditioning. Although the approach is minimalist, the results are extraordinary as *Tahuichi* boasts a fantastic record in the *Mundialito* – one of the premier youth tournaments in South American soccer.

Trained Traits in Unstructured Settings

There are traits that coaches in structured systems try to impart on players as a teachable talent that are requirements for the unstructured, organic game. Traits such as resourcefulness, toughness, leadership, creativity, one-on-one ability, and speed of thought are a few of these traits.

On the other hand, there are attributes that the structured, coached version of the game instills in a player that are difficult to learn in unstructured environments, such as tactical nous, the ability to cooperate with others towards a coach-directed objective, and the organized schemas of technical drills and exercises – performed within the team construct – that align with a club or team's philosophy of playing. This is one reason the game's top-level must be connected to its lower levels in order to fully develop the game on both ends of the spectrum. Tying grassroots football to the top tier creates a clear vision for holistic development.

In the United States, soccer is an increasingly expensive activity – there is no subsidized initiative at the local government level to support a non-pay-to-play system. The cohesion between communities and sport is often found in other sports such as basketball, baseball, and American football, but with soccer it remains disjointed and lacking direction from a governance perspective. Growing up in this system, it was apparent that in most areas where youth soccer was prevalent from an organized perspective – with an abundance of teams, clubs, and tournaments – there was a distinct lack of organic play away from that team dynamic.

Kids rarely regarded playing pick-up games as anything more than horsing around with friends, which isn't the worst thing as fun and free play are important elements that draw us to sport. However, in countries that fail to tie the top tiers of the game with the grassroots levels, there exists a major disconnect when it comes to utilizing the resources and having a clear direction for the overall development of the game, not just player development. This is evident in coaching education, coach and player retention, and clear communication that is age and skill-level specific, to name a few elements.

There is, however, a common player-specific requirement that also takes place. As a player ages and progresses, they must continue to dedicate substantial amounts of time to supplemental training regimens in order to separate themselves from their peers and to maintain or even gain a competitive edge. Inevitably, these players often become *focal points* on the teams they play on because they are able to attain a higher level of play due to the increased time spent playing the game or training towards a specific objective. By consistently getting additional repetitions, these players are sharpening their diverse skillsets, which puts them at a distinct competitive advantage when compared to those relying solely on formalized team training.

"Going to Court"

A few months after playing collegiately, I found myself at the crossroads many players find themselves at – what now? At the time, I was clueless as to what to do next in terms of playing. Professional prospects were not an option, and finding a good men's league team to play on was challenging as good teams were few and far between. Additionally, at 22 years old, if you're not playing professionally, it's not uncommon to wonder what the point of continuing to seek the game out really is. After a lifetime pursuing soccer through disparate pathways, my journey ultimately led to an office job and graduate school.

But, like many players in similar predicaments, I couldn't deny that I missed playing and still loved the game. I missed training with a team; I missed the conditioning, the workouts, the matches, and all the other aspects of being a high-level player. And so, I was so happy when I found a hotbed – hidden in plain sight – while on a run after work one evening.

Midway through that run, I encountered a roller hockey rink full of boisterous people. The squeak of shoes against pavement chirped through the night air. The rink's floodlights illuminated the adjacent softball fields where local pub leagues played. What I saw beyond the chain-linked fence was something I never expected to see in a park that was almost always empty – or so I thought. Other than the odd youth team practice, nobody ever played soccer there. And yet, here it was – with some remarkably high-level soccer being played. I stopped running and watched for a few minutes.

After several minutes of some of the most combative games I'd ever seen take place in a cage, the play came to a brief pause. One of the Hispanic players looked at me and said, "Yo! You wanna play?"

I nodded and responded, "You sure? Yeah, I'll play."

As I made my way to the court off the footpath, it occurred to me they needed a body – a stand-in participant. I had lived this scenario a few times before, so I knew I had to be careful with how I played. What they didn't know was that I wasn't looking to merely participate. I was there to play!

The level of play was high, and the speed of play was even faster as the games were a series of transitions and odd-man breaks. Tackles were high, hard, late, and often cynical. The chain-linked fence gave way with every shoulder barge and hip-check that catapulted a body into it. I figured if I decided to be the playmaker, I would be smashed. If I was too passive, I would be smashed.

There was no avoiding it – contact and combat were inevitable. The competitive side I channeled was not developed on the spot, however. It was forged decades before as a young boy playing in these environments in San Jose, Chicago, and in the Netherlands. The game on this level is truly universal. The street game doesn't care what team you made, how many trophies you won, or how good your parents think you are – all that matters is the *here and now*. Performance, leadership, collaboration, creativity, artistry, and a willingness to compete are the currency of a free game. I adjusted my game to align with the condensed space and aggressiveness of the pressing and tackles. Each play was a quick one-two touch playing sequence. The tempo was simple, pass and move, get the ball back, and look to score or recirculate possession. Defensively, it was tackling with authority and cutting out passing lanes.

The first opportunity that was presented to me, I stuck an opponent with a hard tackle, won the ball, and cracked off a shot that sent the ball into the upper corner of the hockey net beyond a stunned sweeper-keeper. A few of the players were surprised, but there was no fanfare. As soon as the ball was retrieved, the next play started. I didn't know if we were even keeping score. Over the next hour or so, I was the recipient of errant elbows and kicks and a slew of insults in Spanish. This was the version of soccer I loved. We played game after game until one of them informed everyone they had to go to work.

"Go to work?" I asked.

"Yeah. I'm a cook at the Taqueria off County Farm Road, in the plaza," one guy said.

Another chimed in, "My shift starts at the warehouse in 30 minutes. I'm out."

"You come back? Same time tomorrow night?" one of them asked me.

I nodded.

"I'll see you tomorrow night," I said.

I shook hands and bumped fists with most of them and resumed my run. I found it intriguing that these players were factory workers, cooks, busboys, and belonged to maintenance crews within the community, and yet they still found time not just to play, but to compete. These were good players. They may not have been *team* players, but they had the skill, tenacity, and creativity on-par with many of the talented players I had played against and alongside up to this point.

However, for them, the game through the lens I had experienced was different. This court, that "school of hard knocks," these late hours playing in vacant parks beyond operating hours was where they plied their trade. From my perspective, this wasn't glamorous; but I also got the feeling they didn't yearn for anything else. What we did have in common was a love for the game and no other real playing options. That made it perfect.

For a year, we played every night. These cage matches were ruthless. At work, I strapped ice packs to my shins and ankles while I typed away at my keyboard and attended webinars. I could deal with the lack of sleep and dedicated rest because playing like this was totally worth it.

The whole thing was like a scene out of the movie *Fight Club*.

I didn't bother talking about these late-night cage matches to others partly out of a selfishness to keep it a secret for myself, and partly because I knew others wouldn't understand or appreciate it as I did. Plus, it was *my unique experience* that filled a void in the years I was entering: a new stage of life that involved corporate work, graduate school, and defining who I was without a team or coaching staff to direct my playing environment. There remains something beautiful about all of this – the game was finally *mine* again. After a lifetime of training and playing for the opportunities to be coached, to be part of a team, to have my game structured, I returned to the type of game I first played as a boy under a Californian sun.

Exploring the outer edges

These episodes of my playing experience prove that there are thriving pockets of the informal version of the game – hidden in plain sight – that seem simply surreal. In a way, these experiences – where the game is an extension of life and identity – forced me to explore the outer edges of my psyche. To find a way to play, no matter what else is going on, is a unique obsession. Being one of *those* players in the shadows of society that play for pride, and as a matter of self-expression, is an escape from a world of hyper-structure and corporate conformity. For me, nothing else existed when I was playing, and nothing else mattered. For that interval of time, I wasn't a corporate employee; I wasn't anything or anyone except a player pursuing his passion – if only for an hour or two.

I still wonder how young players view pick-up soccer. As each generation passes, the talent and skill level rises, but what seems to be missing are those intangibles needed to elevate and apply those skills. Personally, finding a game on television when I was growing up was rare. To make up for this, my friends and I snuck into pubs to watch games from England, Germany, Spain, or Italy purchased on Pay-Per-View or bandit-broadcast with a modified cable box. The fond memories of immediately running outside after watching replays of World Cup 1990, 1994, and 1998 and the 1999 Women's World Cup games on VHS tapes – trying to emulate and master what was recorded – are treasured experiences forged in my memories.

Years on, this resourcefulness is as important a skill as any on the field. For example, when I was 14, my good friend, Tristan, and I found buddies to play with every day after school, at the local fields. It honestly didn't matter if we were in the snow, rain, sleet, or darkness; we would find or create a game. We played jumpers for goalposts, and "three bar," and invented games that didn't require teams where each player was against everyone else in a free-for-all. One game we made up required us to score by hitting the side netting outside of the six-yard box – all other goals didn't count! These games honed unique skills we automatically deployed in structured competition.

Perhaps making the game a lifestyle and amassing thousands of touches on the ball each day became a training ritual. I wanted to wear the panels off the ball, so my parents would buy me a new one. There remains an allure to this game of shadows where kits, line-ups, and formalities are of little significance, and all that matters is the present moment, and the ultimate imperative is "next goal wins."

CHAPTER 14: EARN THIS

Growing up, I had a Bolivian friend named Sebastian. We attended the same school in San Jose, California. We also played on the same club team, but we were more than teammates – we were best friends.

Sebastian's family lived on the other side of town during the "dot-com boom" in the burgeoning Silicon Valley of northern California. To complicate matters, along with our friendship, his parents were in the middle of a messy divorce. I'd often go weeks without seeing Sebastian, who spent the majority of his time with his mother. During the summer months, I spent several days with him each week while my parents worked. Prior to moving to the United States, Sebastian was a player in what is known as the *Tahuichi* academy in Santa Cruz, Bolivia.

Sebastian and his older brother, Giovanni, were born and raised in the lower-middle class in Bolivia – just above what could be considered categorically impoverished. One of the first things I noticed was Sebastian and Gio rarely played in shoes. They complained that shoes hurt their feet, and they could not "feel" the ball. While that may have been true, I think they avoided playing in shoes because they were expensive for their family, and they didn't want to risk getting them dirty or, worse, stolen. Gio was 16-years-old and was a fiery individual on and off the field. His skill level was decent, but what he lacked in skill he made up for in tenacity and aggression. Gio played in a way that forced opposing players into mistakes. He was street-smart and savvy in his positioning and style of play.

Sebastian, however, was a different class of player. As a playmaker, Sebastian saw scenarios develop several steps ahead of time. His creativity in one-on-one scenarios made him a special player. He saw the action on the pitch unfolding before most other players, and his play elevated everyone else's level. For a young player, his speed of play was highlighted by the weight of each pass, which allowed him to use his vision to unlock teams.

During those summer days I spent with them, Gio usually walked with us to a local park, often teasing us and threatening to punt our ball over a fence or stab it with a box-cutter he carried in his pocket. As a teenager with a rebellious side, Gio was into a multitude of activities that seemed to tap into his upbringing in the *barrios* in Bolivia. When Sebastian and I were ten-years-old, we noticed Gio acting differently. His temper was incendiary, and he would often show up with cuts and bruises from fist-fights. Sebastian told me that Gio was *initiated* into a local gang "for protection" and that the initiation process involved being mobbed and beaten by other members of the gang in a test of resilience and survival. Gio was also undeterred by conflict and prone to commit petty crimes such as shoplifting or vandalizing property with his other friends.

Over the next two years, Gio struggled to channel his ability in soccer, and his ambition waned. However, Gio kept us out of trouble. When Gio smoked cigarettes and joints and drank with his friends or involved himself in local gang skirmishes, he made sure Sebastian was free and clear from that lifestyle. Gio knew Sebastian possessed a passion and talent for the game stemming from his time at *Tahuichi*, which kept Sebastian on a path of relentless training on his own or with me.

By the time Sebastian's parents divorced, he and Gio moved to a small apartment in a rough part of the city. The family grew increasingly worried whenever Gio hadn't been home in a few days, but it soon became clear Gio could not be controlled. At the time, I was 12-years-old and learning the various degrees and contexts of sporting-based competition, whether it was playing in high-level youth leagues or playing against tough players at local parks and courts in an area where the demographic was diverse in class and race.

I obviously played organized soccer in local leagues, which was great for my development. But the other side of my game that developed took place in the neighborhood streets and parks. Pick-up games often became after-school battles. On the way home, we found games at the local courts at the park. Backpacks and lunchboxes became goalposts, and inevitably, scuffles and punch-ups ensued as tempers boiled over. The competitive fire of the street game brought out our worst attitudes, but oftentimes, it brought out our best soccer.

One day, without Gio walking with us to the park, we grew restless and the heat of the small apartment forced us out. We walked to a park near the apartment they relocated to, and one that I had never been to before. There, a group of teenagers meandered around the plot of land and took to violently throwing the rocks off the dusty plot towards a nearby highway before starting a pick-up game. The park was unkempt. Thick patches of crabgrass littered the dirt square as the seasonal drought in northern California turned fields to dustbowls. Between the thick sprouts of two-spike crabgrass, the "field" was littered with rocks, discarded newspapers, empty beer bottles, and countless cigarette butts. The group yelled at each other and threw dirt at the smaller kids. At a nearby picnic table, a group of men passed joints and cigarettes, and pulled from bottles of liquor – cackling and arguing in Spanish.

Sebastian and I kicked a ball around before one of the teenage boys whistled over to us. I asked Sebastian if he knew the boys, and he nodded apprehensively. The vibrant orange hue of the afternoon sun illuminated his chestnut-colored eyes as he sized up the other players before whispering, "Gio knows them. They're mean."

Anxiety overtook me. Sebastian was a tough kid, and I thought I was, too. What threw me off was the change in Sebastian's attitude. He morphed from footballer to cage fighter – bouncing up and down, popping his neck side-to-side, posturing as if he was about to throw down as he slipped off his shoes. I looked at Sebastian, whose eyes locked onto the group while I bent down to tie my shoe.

"Take off your shoes," Sebastian insisted as I stared at him in bewilderment as he took his own shoes off. "No way," I said, "put your shoes back on."

"Take them off," Sebastian said through clenched teeth as he stormed over and began untying my shoes aggressively before I hastily slipped them off myself. Grabbing my shoes and socks and shoving them into his backpack, Sebastian signaled for me to shut my mouth. He ran over to a row of hedges and shoved the backpack underneath the thorny bushes.

"They'll take your shoes," Sebastian said as he let out an ear-piercing whistle that caught me off-guard to get the attention of a large group of locals kicking the ball around. Initially, I thought Sebastian was overreacting. My main worry wasn't about shoes; it was about getting mugged by the group. I didn't speak fluent Spanish, so I had no choice but to follow his lead as we walked up to the group. The teams were divvied up haphazardly. I was picked last.

Sebastian talked with the others and joked around until he realized I wasn't on his team. A few hurried sentences turned into an argument, and plenty of finger-pointing in my direction, followed by some pushing and shoving before one of the teenagers grabbed my arm and switched places with me, kicking dirt at me during the exchange. I felt a rush of anxiety as I received glares from the others. "They have their shoes on!" I complained as I looked at the other players' shoes, which were tattered, off-brand, and nothing like the nicer shoes we just hid under the thorny bushes.

"Shut up and just play. Watch yourself," Sebastian said.

The game started, and the first pass my way resulted in the ball bouncing over my foot as I caught an elbow to my solar plexus. The pass was errant; the elbow to my sternum was not. I should have seen that coming. As the target of late tackles, cheap shots, and verbal abuse, my concentration wavered as the players whistled and cajoled, and the drunks at the table laughed and jeered. I felt queasy and debated leaving, but decided to play out of fear of leaving Sebastian stranded.

For Sebastian, this was more than a game. He lived there and didn't have the luxury of leaving as I did. We used tree stumps as goals. Even though the field was a rough patch, I focused on playing fast. To me, playing barefoot felt strange. My soles shot with pain with every step. Sebastian, on the other hand, played like a specter floating over tackles. He cradled the ball with deft touches and seemed to bounce and bound off the ground like a gazelle.

Playing barefoot forced us both to play quickly and simply. Playing slowly invited getting your feet stepped on. To the other players, it didn't matter that we played barefoot. It seemed to me that their intent was to maim. It was evident that we weren't playing against talented players who trained or knew how to defend well. What we were playing against was a collection of tough teenagers who played a different brand of the game reliant on physicality.

Every time Sebastian received the ball, he either passed to me or dribbled at a back-peddling opponent, using a body feint or a shoulder dip to shift them off-balance. At that moment, I realized something that was never obvious before – Sebastian was using the rough pitch to his advantage by collecting the ball and dribbling right at a player, forcing them to defend on the uneven surface.

When the ball came to me, I did the same thing and played at a pace they could not defend. The game brought out a swagger in us. This type of game was not uncommon for me. The difference, this time, was I was playing on the other side of town with a heavy gang presence, without my shoes, and without Gio to help us in case things went south. My play morphed into something automatic. I was accessing and retrieving countless experiences, one-on-one duels, and opportunities from playing pick-up games for much of my life. Additionally, I had refined my technical ability by playing on a high-level club team and, tactically, it helped tremendously as I knew when to commit to a tackle and when to track a runner.

After a while, the game became less about winning and more about humiliating the opponent. A thick layer of dust and sweat-induced mud caked my feet as the sun disappeared over the foothills. The last goal involved me retrieving the ball from out of bounds as players on the other team chomped at my feet and ankles, clearly refusing to acknowledge the boundaries – so I kept dribbling. I passed to Sebastian, who stepped on the ball and rolled it back to me as I overlapped him. For a few minutes, we played what can only be described as barefoot, dirt patch *tiki-taka* before I slid the ball between the last player's legs even though I had the option to simply dribble around him and slammed the ball against the tree stump.

Game over.

The defending player, an older and much larger guy, walked over to me and spat in my face before letting loose with a punch that landed above my right eye before he shoved me to the ground. "Fuck you!" he said, kicking dirt in my face, and kicking me in the gut again before his friends subdued him. As I rolled on the ground, my right temple and eye throbbed like it had its own heartbeat. The others laughed. The incident set me off.

I had never seethed with this much anger before. The altercation was a defining moment for me. It remains my baptism of *barrio* soccer in spit and dust rather than holy water. Rage surged through my veins as I shot up, throwing haymakers at the guy who'd hit me. He fell off-balance in a heap on the ground. I started stamping and kicking him before Sebastian, and a few others, grabbed me and stopped the melee. The table of jeering drunkards whistled and laughed.

I stormed over to a redwood tree stump and inspected my feet, brushing the dirt and grime off them, smearing it across my forehead as I wiped the sweat off my eyebrow. My lower lip quivered, and I did my best not to cry as the metallic taste of my own blood filled my mouth.

Smirking, Sebastian walked over to me and put his arm around me. "You shouldn't have fought him. But I'm glad you did. They thought you cheated by going out of bounds," he said. I remained silent and just stared at my feet, which were unrecognizable.

"Good."

That was all I could say.

The breeze kicked up more dust. Sebastian and I waited for the others to leave before walking over to the bush to retrieve the bag. A large, toothy grin widened across Sebastian's face as he shot his hand into the bush and retrieved the bag, holding it like a fisherman holding the day's catch. We walked home barefoot, kicking the ball back and forth. When I got back to Sebastian's apartment, his father called my parents to come get me. They inspected my wounds and told me to wash my feet.

That day at the park changed me. I experienced my first real fight and gained a newfound swagger in my step. Additionally, I found that

I *could* play differently if I was barefoot — faster, more technically, and with closer control.

The Tahuichi Way

What was it that made Tahuichi different? When Bolivia qualified for the 1994 World Cup, its first World Cup appearance in 44 years, many were stunned. It seemed Bolivia came out of nowhere, but that notion could not be farther from the truth. Bolivian stars like Jaime Moreno, Marco 'El Diablo' Etcheverry, Erwin Sanchez, Luis Cristaldo, and a collection of other young, talented players took the footballing world by storm in the 1990s. The common link between them was that they were all products of the fabled *Tahuichi Academy*.

Based in Bolivia's hinterlands, located north of Serranías Chiquitanas towards the Brazilian border, the academy opened its doors in 1978. Its objectives were simple: to teach soccer, resist poverty, and give a fighting chance to the poorest of Bolivia's sons.

In an interview with FIFA.com, Moreno recalled his time at the academy. "Those years, and Tahuichi in general, meant everything to me and everyone involved in Bolivian football." Moreno, who went on to be capped 75 times for *Los Altiplanicos*, credited the academy with his success, "Everything we achieved was learned there."

From the beginning of their journey in the game, Jaime Moreno and much of the rest of the Bolivian golden generation played, lived, and trained together from their early teenage years until they went on to become the spine of a Bolivian side that proved to be unbeatable at home in La Paz and reached the Copa America final in 1997.

"When we were with Tahuichi, we traveled all over Europe and the United States. We learned to win together and be better and bigger than we ever thought we could be," Moreno said. The environment at Tahuichi proved to be pivotal in the development of the players in Bolivia. "We were hungrier than most. When you have to go through the hard stuff in life, it makes you stronger. If you don't have that hunger and things get hard, you might just quit. Sometimes things can come too easy — they didn't come easy for us players who came through Tahuichi."

Sebastian and I played on a team coached by a man named Armando Mendoza. Armando was also a product of Tahuichi's academy and arrived in northern California on a college soccer scholarship. He knew American kids lacked a dedicated footballing culture. Naturally, he and Sebastian were on the same wavelength, and he used Sebastian to help bridge the cultural gap. Armando's coaching style was unconventional – it represented the Tahuichi way.

Our training sessions began with breathing exercises. We sat down and inhaled through our noses, holding the air in our lungs, and exhaled slowly through our mouths. A single breath would last ten seconds. Armando rolled his index fingers in a circular manner in front of his face to demonstrate the cyclical motion of the air entering and exiting our bodies.

When we didn't take the exercise seriously, Armando yelled, "No talking! Breathe from the belly!" placing his hand on his abdomen to demonstrate how this type of breathing should originate from the belly, not the chest. Practices took place at a park that had an ankle-deep stream circulating around the perimeter. The park was littered with sand volleyball courts, baseball fields, and a few poorly-maintained soccer fields. After the breathing exercises, we shed our socks and shoes and followed Armando to the little stream, where he instructed us to run laps in the cool water.

Onlookers stared in confusion as we sloshed our way around the park like a group of wild beasts, laughing and splashing each other. A few kids took to tripping others up, so they landed face-first in the water. The first lap was always unnatural but the subsequent laps were energetic foot races. Two players sat in the stream back-to-back and, at a signal, both players shot up and took off, the trailing player giving chase to the rabbit – the objective was to turn and make up the distance while the leading player with the advantage worked on his first few explosive steps. Armando's sessions challenged us, and running through water proved to be an effective way for a bunch of wild kids to bond while gaining fitness.

Other exercises placed us in pairs to climb on one another's backs while running a series of sprints up and down a small hill. In addition to gaining strength and balance, it also taught us the importance of working for your teammate. Nobody wanted to fail their teammate, which began to translate to our play on the pitch. After some sessions, we played barefoot in the sand volleyball pits and on the cinder baseball outfields to toughen our feet up and improve our touch. Initially, the sloppiness of our passes would have appalled even the worst teams in the area. The objective was to dribble and pass with more variation, creativity, and at a quicker pace. We learned how to scoop the ball, flick it on, and how to take up good starting positions and passing lanes for one another.

This organic training paired well with Armando's creativity as a coach. However, he also knew that this unconventional training was only a piece of the puzzle. We needed structure and organization tactically, and of course, we needed competition. After destroying our first few opponents in our local league, Armando pulled us from the league. He knew we wouldn't develop as a team, and so we competed in the higher level league in an age group several years older than us in the Umberto Abronzino division of the South San Jose Soccer League. This level was more competitive and combative than the leagues in which we were accustomed to playing. Games had a similar intensity to the pick-up soccer turf wars… without the frequency of the fights. But what we needed to learn was not how to fight, but how to compete. Tactically, we were picked apart by superior opposition. Physically, we were outmatched. When a player on our team decided to dribble when he should have passed, or passed when he should have switched the play, we were punished. This was what we needed.

At first, we got demolished in every area of play. However, as a collective, we refused to remain in a lower division where we wouldn't be challenged. The learning curve at this higher level was steep. We tried to keep the ball on the surface and isolate players we thought were the weakest link on the other teams. We tried to implement tactics and create numerical advantages when we had the ball, such as turning a spell in possession into a 4v2 or 2v1 situation. Although our fitness was superior to many of our opponents, these players had played more games as individuals, and as a collective, and had amassed more experience. Away from the matches, the unconventional training proved transformative and allowed us to play more creatively.

A Cold Chicago Welcome

The following year, my family moved from northern California to suburban Chicago. I missed Sebastian and my friends. In this new place, I spent plenty of time training alone, after school, kicking a ball alone against a field house wall for hours. The game was popular, but it was also different culturally. Soccer was just another sport that kids played in the Midwest. Whereas it was *the* sport we played in California. My father found a few teams for me to play on, but finding new friends proved more difficult, which is to be expected in a move across the country at 13-years-old. I did find playing indoors during the Illinois winters enjoyable, but admittedly, it was a completely alien game to me. I enjoyed exposing the clumsiness of others and the chaos from using the walls for fun; it was a frenetic and chaotic kick-ball exchange. Physically, players here were more athletic, stronger, and clumsier than the skilled players I grew up playing with and against in California. These were teenagers who played hockey, American football, and baseball and who were physically developing into powerful athletes, not skilled soccer players. That being said, these players in the Midwest weren't bad. In fact, they were talented and more direct, having grown up playing in organized and coached environments. I knew playing in these environments was important for my development and socialization.

After a good individual performance at a holiday break tournament, an athletic-looking man approached my father as I sat on the bench, taking off my shoes. My new teammates never cooled down after games, but instead ran off to meet their mothers waiting in minivans to take them off to eat pizza or go to the next sporting event. Seeing players just leave after a game was weird – they couldn't wait to get away from soccer.

My father and this man talked for over an hour, and I ended walking back on the turf and played on my own, barefoot. The rough field turf felt strange on my feet, but I had developed a comfort for getting technical work without my shoes on.

I continued working with the ball, dribbling against invisible players on the empty field and passing the ball against the wall hundreds of times until my father called me over to tell me he had "great news." The man he spoke with was a coach visiting Chicago from Dallas, Texas. He was there to watch some players on the other team. He told me he admired my poise on the ball and ability to pass and control the tempo of the play and extended me an invitation to join his team heading over to Europe to play friendly matches, and train with professional academy teams, while participating in two popular youth tournaments in Denmark and Sweden.

Naturally, I was flattered, but I was also scared. I immediately agreed to go because I thought my father would accompany me. On the way home, he told me, "It's going to be you and only you going." My heart sank, but he also told me the opportunity was a special one. My father never put unnecessary pressure on me, but he did challenge me to fully commit to whatever it was I pursued. It could have been any discipline, but this was my sport and he encouraged me to learn and push myself well past my comfort zone. As I stared out of the window on the way home, I thought about how many of my friends in California would never leave those dusty park fields or cracked concrete courts to play. They would never get a chance to be selected to play for a team assembled to compete in two international tournaments while training with academy teams in professional environments.

In my father, I saw a man dedicated to his work and family. As an elite swimmer in his college years, my father dedicated thousands of hours to his training in the pool. He would often encourage me only to raise the bar just a bit higher – challenging me to improve to the point it seemed like I could never do enough.

I stressed about going to Europe for a few reasons. The first was about my ability. I had no idea what I would encounter in terms of talent on the team I was blindly joining to travel abroad. Secondly, the level of play there would be far superior to anything in my experiences at home. Finally, I stressed because deep down I knew we couldn't really afford the trip. To alleviate this concern, my father worked a corporate job that required him to leave the house at six in the morning. He worked until 5 p.m. and then took a job working nights and weekends at a sporting goods store to make ends meet. My parents worked tirelessly so my sisters and I could have high-level opportunities in sport.

The weeks ticked by and, to prepare for Europe, I oscillated from team to team. The goal was to play in as many games while getting as many training sessions as possible. I played indoor, outdoor, in ethnic leagues, and joined random pick-up games with strangers. I spent most nights dribbling the ball through my neighborhood streets getting thousands of touches on the ball and working on different techniques.

Looking back, the challenges I faced were more social than anything else. Most players on each of these teams had cliques. After all, they grew up playing together. I was the outsider, the youngster, the mercenary in the making looking for games. To them, I was taking one of their game-day roster spots. I focused purely on playing. My adolescent attitude began to emerge, too. My experiences and the impending trip abroad dominated my thought processes and behavior. At one session, a player refused to pass the ball to me during a scrimmage, for which we paid the price in the form of sprints – a form of punishment that I learned was normal.

Eventually, I lost my cool and confronted a player who was at least five years older than me. The exchange led to a shoving match before he punched me in the gut and tossed me to the ground. The coach and team watched and smirked as the two of us ran sprints. Whoever finished last in a series of sprints was made to repeat the punishment.

Part of me relished the punishment and taunted the other player during the sprints. I had developed an edge that was getting sharper by the training session. However, no matter what I did, I seemed to create enemies within the team, and it wasn't down to soccer. It was down to socially not fitting in, with an element of bullying. In hindsight, my behavior was dictated by ignorant and arrogant adolescence in full bloom. That team's particular coach told my father I wasn't welcome back, which was fine with me.

Soon after, I felt I was being punished when my father insisted I join another U-18 team at 13-years-old. Not only was I young and frustrated, but these players were physically-developed. They fit the "bigger, faster, stronger" ethos of American youth sports. I spent week after week training and playing with this older team, literally getting the shit kicked out of me on a regular basis. The coach was named Greg Muhr; he was a former professional player in the old North American Soccer League (NASL) and Major Indoor Soccer League (MISL). He was unlike any coach I ever had. He spoke with authority and led by example, each session.

Greg knew how to handle a 13-year-old with attitude and talent. He never kept the wolves at bay, but in a way he was always in control. He didn't bail me out of tough situations, nor did he allow anything to get out of hand. It was good experience and mix of great coaching, intense sessions, and social development courtesy of a man who had played professionally with and against some great players. Greg Muhr was pivotal in my development and didn't put up with any bullshit lash-outs and immaturity. He warned me about being governed by emotions as my play continued to improve. As spring gave way to summer, I was playing no fewer than six days a week with three different teams at three different age groups.

There came a point when I took the intensity from training with the older guys and unleashed it on players my age. My temperament was a factor, but my overall development and level of play soared. The trade-off was frightening to some degree. The game controlled my attitude and social interactions – almost to a fault. At school, I ran my hands up and down my shins, counting the bumps and contusions. People at school asked me if I had been in a fight; in many ways, I had.

My competitiveness burned ferociously and I began to see, in myself, what the older players I grew up watching exuded. In many respects, this period of development sharpened me up and turned me into a different human being. Every training session with the older team became a cauldron of competition. The confrontations were the result of a competitive playing environment aimed to mold a player the way nature shapes a wild animal – fight or perish. Stories like this are in world football. Players like Arturo Vidal, Luis Suarez, Enner Valencia, Alexis Sanchez, to name a few, experienced upbringings where their backs were constantly against the wall.

Martin Domin of the *Daily Mail* wrote about Vidal's poverty and subsequent habit-formation that resulted from his circumstances.

"Had it not been for a leading racehorse trainer, Arturo Vidal may never have fulfilled his potential as a footballer. From the age of nine, he would skip school, hop on his bicycle and pedal the six miles to Santiago's racetrack. There, he would feed the horses and muck out their stables; all the time keeping a close eye on the money in his pocket that he had collected from his neighbors. Before the racing started, he sought out a grown-up to place bets for him as his friends and family waited back home in the community of San Joaquin.

"Deep down, however, he knew his legs were too long for him to realize his dream of being a jockey and that his only equine options were to attempt to make his fortune by gambling or to keep looking after the horses in his care.

"But his boss, Enrique Carreno, had seen Vidal playing with a ball and took him to the side one day. 'This is not for you, kid,' he said. 'You have a future in football.'"

Earn This

It is clear that my upbringing conditioned me to form several defensive mechanisms, such as aggression and intensity. However, those remain response-based aspects of competition. The skill developed by playing in different environments, training with repetition, and acquiring a high volume of both formal and informal competitive games unearthed new opportunities. The training, though, remained a key factor as it helped immensely to have exceptionally skilled and hyper-competitive teammates and coaches who created training environments that mimicked meaningful competition.

On Greg Muhr's team, his approach and intensity allowed us to treat game days as opportunities to showcase what we had put into the training, which was often much more intense than match play. By the time we took the field against an opponent, we eventually learned to switch off the malice and perform for one another. I eventually came to terms that this was a variation of the pick-up games I played in San Jose. I also had to change as a player. No longer could I rely on the pick-up games of my childhood to pull from every time things got challenging. I knew there was no going back.

As a former professional player, Greg taught me more about being a player than anyone else. He reiterated that if I wanted to truly improve, I had to accept the reality that conditioning myself to play faster and simpler was only part of the learning curve for players in more advanced and challenging environments.

Europe

The day we left for the European trip, my father gave me a card and some cash. We didn't have much money, and I felt undeserving when my parents gave me what felt like so much money. The card was beautiful and simple, but what stuck with me was the last part. My father ended the card with the phrase: "Earn this."

I repeated the phrase over and over. I vowed to play my best and make the most of the experience. The flight to Europe took me from Chicago to Minneapolis, from Minneapolis to Oslo, and from Oslo to Gothenburg. In Gothenburg, I took a ferry south to Frederikshavn for a tournament called Dana Cup. The rest of the team flew to Denmark directly from Dallas and awaited my arrival.

By the time I arrived, I was jet-lagged and disorientated. I passed out during the formal introductions. After an injection of glucose and a steady diet of sugar tablets and orange juice, I trained with my new teammates before our first match. The July afternoons under Denmark's blue skies were a sight to behold. Taking the field for the opening game at one of Europe's largest youth tournaments was fantastic. In the chaos of getting to Europe to meet a new team, I paid no attention to the schedule. I just showed up ready to play.

For our first game, the opposing team was late to the field. As we warmed up and got into our pre-game huddle, we heard a group chanting. A small mob of players wearing vibrant yellow and green uniforms waved flags as they made their way to the field. I looked up at the scoreboard as the word "TAHUICHI" appeared. Deep down, part of me felt that I knew what Tahuichi represented. I trusted that my experiences with Sebastian and Armando prepared me for this game.

The Tahuichi U-18s beat us 3-1. It could have been more. Their superior technique was matched by their composure on the ball, and their defense in one-on-one duels was fantastic. They pressed as a collective. The team I played for was very good, but we had barely trained together, and nothing could have prepared us for this opponent. The Tahuichi team used its fitness and speed to attack quickly in transition. By the time we developed a rhythm and established possession, the game was over.

After the game, we sat with the Bolivian players and enjoyed a small meal and some conversation. For many of my teammates, the skill and fitness of the opponent fascinated them to the point of envy and frustration. I remember thinking we came all the way to Europe to get dismantled by a team from South America. The victors were humble. There was no gloating, no excessive celebrations, no arrogance.

Their coach told us players in Santa Cruz are often spotted in a local kick-around. By the time many of these players enter the academy, they haven't owned a pair of boots. The more they spoke of their home, it was obvious they were proud of their home. Each player proudly showed us cracked and folded pictures of the rust-covered tin rooftops of their homes. The Bolivians continued to tell us how they trained each day. Although I had an idea, I was enthralled to listen. As one individual told me one part of his training regimen, another player chimed in explaining how they run miles in shallow creek beds being careful not to step into a hidden pit or roll an ankle on a smooth stone; about how they run up and down the sand dunes for hours, sometimes carrying a teammate on their backs.

I smiled and thought of Armando and Sebastian. I also thought of Gio and wondered if he ever found his way in life. The afternoon gave way to evening, and we continued sharing pictures of our homes and families and eventually made our way back to the dormitory with a shoddy internet connection so we could send emails home. I mentioned my friend, Sebastian, and my former coach, hoping to strike up a connection with the players, but they hadn't heard of them. For these players, the tournament was less of a trip abroad and more of an audition to hopefully be scouted by a European team. For us, the trip was about gaining experience.

That night, players from other teams stayed inside to play cards and watch movies. The Bolivians were absent from the card tables and players' lounges. Instead, they gathered outside to play barefoot on the smooth concrete of a nearby square – juggling the ball and performing tricks and flicks in small groups. Anyone from the other teams at the tournament – who passed by – received an invite to join them. Before long, players from different nationalities, abilities, and upbringings were kicking their shoes off and joining in the celebration of football and friendship. Their appetite for the game was infectious, but their willingness to include and meet others in their version of the game is one of many reasons this sport is called "The Beautiful Game."

CHAPTER 15: GODS OF THE GRITTY ARENA

In training, the soccer scrimmage form must be used most of the time, just as in street soccer. In this form, it is essential to once again play real soccer. This develops a combination of technical, tactical, physical, and mental qualities.

Rinus Michels, FIFA Coach of the Century

Chicago's winter climate changes people. The cold is heavy, but it's the wind ripping through people that affects the way they live, socialize, and train. When I first moved to Chicago, I enjoyed the cold. The regular snowfall, the iced-over ponds, the sledding, the whole reality of winter excited me. After a few years of living through these winters, I realized the importance of training and adjusting my mindset during those cold and dark months.

On some level, moving across the country helped me adapt to a world of changes. I had to seek out teams to play on, find new friends, and prepare for the game at higher levels in a variety of settings, both outdoors and indoors. Around this time, I played on several teams and adapted my style of play to each environment. By the time I turned 17, I played for the area's best club team and in the competitive men's leagues on two Latino teams and one Polish team.

Socially, it helped that I made several friends from all walks of life. On the Latino and Polish teams, most of the players were older and continued to find ways to play around Chicago, where many of them lived and worked an assortment of blue-collar jobs, such as laboring or manufacturing. My family lived in a small town to the west of the city, so when I wanted to play or train with these adult teams, I would take the train to the city and enter a different world to organized youth club soccer – the world which I knew.

As dedicated as I was, I still had a way to go in terms of my own development. Nonetheless, I knew that the best way to improve was to get as many games in as I could. As much as I needed training sessions, I needed to play in more games. The club team I played for was well-coached and well-stocked with great youth players – many of whom would go on to play professionally. To be honest, that environment proved to be incredibly valuable because – on any given day – I could see where I ranked among players in my age bracket and talent pool.

However, the experiences of my upbringing and soccer travel abroad conditioned me to become a searcher. For some players, it is not enough to just play a few days a week at organized practice and a game over the weekend. I was at an age of adventure and self-discovery, and the sport was my vehicle between different cultural and sporting worlds. One of the most valuable lessons I continued to learn revolved around the importance of recognizing the different codes for each environment. Each team had a different set of ethics. Whilst I could dribble freely on my club team, I would have to pass the ball quickly on the Polish team. Where I would avoid retribution with my club team, I felt obligated to seek it out on the Latino teams.

Competition often comes down to personal pride. One's willingness to compete is often less about the outcome of a game and more about an overarching principle. I saw this in my experiences playing with my friend Sebastian in rough pick-up games. The pride of passing the ball with excellence to help a teammate look good, or to approach the game with the right competitive mentality, became pillars of my playing identity. My obsession with excellence tested my maturity often, and with ferocity at times. Such a mindset, if not harnessed and trained carefully, will lead to the wrong outcomes.

I saw this when I moved to Chicago. My tenacity and overzealousness on the pitch were borne from an upbringing playing the game as an extension of life and my identity. So, when I stumbled onto a neighborhood team – having moved away from all I knew in California to a player pool of individuals who did not honor the game as I did – the result was socially catastrophic but cathartic with regard to my development as a player. Had I dropped my standard of play to "fit in," I would have done myself no favors.

Over the years, I became a journeyman seeking the game out. That sense of adventure appealed to me, and a journey of self-exploration fueled my passion to play. One winter day, while waiting for a ride home after an indoor game near Chicago's South Side, I passed the time by smashing a ball against a rotted wooden backboard on a set of cracked tennis courts near a condemned lot. The Chicago wind tore through the frigid air, but I didn't mind. The gusts invigorated me. Plus, I had to stay outside since the game location was a fieldhouse that happened to look like every other warehouse, and I didn't want my parents to miss the address. So, I thought it best just to play outside and wait with a ball at my foot.

When kicking the ball off the wobbly backboard became boring, I juggled the ball and did some dribbling patterns against invisible opponents. I could feel the eyes of the construction crew and the landscapers watching me. Being a Sunday afternoon, I thought it odd to see crews working. Soon, a group of workers approached me. "Yep, they're kicking me off the site," I said to myself.

But they didn't kick me off. Instead, they asked to play. Their thick accents did not hinder their near-fluent English. These were men in their late-twenties, early-to-mid-thirties. As they congregated, we juggled in a circle before breaking off into a small three-a-side game. Their deft and controlled touches on the ball in steel-toe work boots astounded me. These guys could play. They passed and moved with pace and precision. Then, my parents arrived. Before I left, they invited me to play on their men's team that played in a night league in Chicago, but with one caveat – I had to attend training two nights a week.

Immediately, I accepted. I did not even consider the logistics of the arrangement. That sense of adventure and obsession with the game pulled me in again. One of the workers stressed the seriousness of the training aspect. He wrote down the location of a warehouse on Chicago's Lower West Side near Bridgeport on a small card and said, "When you get there, ask for me at the front desk. My name is Jerzy."

The fact these guys played on a men's league team that trained fascinated me, and so I agreed to show up. Naturally, my parents looked confused as to why I played outside in the cold with a construction crew instead of staying inside the facility. I explained the invitation to them, and my mother immediately objected. My father looked hesitant but intrigued. He knew how much playing meant to me and agreed to take me to the first session the following week.

My father accompanied me, but he remained silent. We shared an understanding that I would negotiate my way through these obscure playing scenarios, and he would be there to support me in any way he could. We walked in to find no front desk to "check-in" at. Inside, a group of steely-eyed Polish men played cards at a small folding table. When they noticed us, they approached and asked, "Who are you?"

I mentioned Jerzy's name on the soccer team, but they just muttered in Polish among themselves. Sensing I showed up to the wrong place, I mentioned a few of the other players from the impromptu three-a-side game, "I met some guys named Pawel, Grzegorz, Zbigniew, and Bartosz."

Their faces remained locked as their jaw muscles tightened. I thought to myself, "What am I doing here?"

My heart sunk and my face flushed with embarrassment as I began stuttering and planning to make my exit back to the car. I began to dig through my pockets to find the address until one of the men broke into a toothy grin, and the rest burst into laughter and said, "Man, you're bad at Polish names!" before offering his hand for me to shake. We discussed soccer for a few minutes before they told me about the requirements of their training facility and team.

The first condition stipulated I could not invite anyone unless Jerzy agreed. Secondly, I could not tell anyone about the gym (I began to think this was Chicago's version of Fight Club). Lastly, I had to work as a courier distributing fliers and marketing collateral for the gym's proprietor around specified neighborhoods. This meant I had to find a way to staple and distribute a predetermined stack of fliers written in a language I could not speak or read, each week, to people at set locations, and paste or staple others at set addresses. In return, I gained access to the facility, and I would receive some pocket cash.

My father looked at Jerzy and the crew and then whispered in my ear, "It's up to you."

I accepted more out of intrigue than anything else. It didn't take me long to figure out the scope of my new job. One day, I asked what the fliers said. The group murmured to themselves before Jerzy told me, "They are church times on the top and business messages on the bottom. We love God. He is very important to us, but we must tell others about our business. You help us with the papers."

I nodded. It didn't really matter to me. What mattered was playing and training with a group of guys that had an edge and appetite for the game that was missing in my club training.

The "fliers" turned out to be advertisements and betting tips for horse racing and European football leagues, along with "unlisted" job listings for contracting work around the area. The last part, the job listings, were the real currency I carried around the routes. As contractors needed temporary or day work, they looked to hire skeleton crews of subcontractors – my role was to get the job leads to specific neighborhoods and shops.

Not being Polish myself was supposed to be an advantage as I traveled through the different ethnic sectors of the route. The gym itself was obviously a front for some under-the-table business ventures. It didn't take a genius to realize they wanted someone who didn't speak the language for the task.

The converted steel pressing warehouse contained a crude version of a gym constructed for dynamic workouts. The squat racks looked like monoliths of a world quarried from iron ore. Rickety stationary bikes, mismatched free weights, and creatively-constructed sandbags were everywhere – but there was no sign of any soccer court or training area. The entire place looked as though it was put together in a day or two.

There were giant tractor tires, Olympic weight sets with rubber bumper plates, a giant wall with X's made of duct tape at the gym's south end. The floor smelled of dried sweat and spoiled milk, the kind found in elementary school cafeterias. At two corners of the gym were giant steel industrial-sized fans that chopped the air and circulated the smells evenly across the place; they distorted the radio playing overhead, and drowned out all conversations.

At the base of the wall was an assortment of rubber and leather medicine balls and a few scuffed soccer balls. The west end had a running strip where lifters and athletes jogged back and forth. The second floor had a small boxing ring, various heavy punching bags, and an assortment of those iron bowling ball-shaped objects with handles – kettlebells.

I was told, "Workout whenever you like. Just don't get hurt."

That seemed simple enough. I walked around the weight sets and the dumbbell rack and just did the workouts I knew. After the session, a man named Piotr handed me the week's stack of fliers for me to distribute. The next time I showed up, I saw Jerzy and the rest of the guys. They immediately took the dumbbells out of my hand, replacing them with a kettlebell. The challenge with working out with kettlebells is that your center of gravity is off-balance, so handling them for a novice like me was awkward.

I applied chalk to my hands and started with a light kettlebell. Jerzy taught me how to perform a series of swings, rotations, and presses with the iron-handled bells. After a warm-up that felt like a workout, I joined them for one of the most intense training sessions I had ever participated in. We worked in circuits of swings, pushes, and pulls with the kettlebells, ranging in intensity and tempo. In any given workout, we amassed anywhere from 500-1,000 swing variations.

For recovery, we performed push-ups and leg lifts. At the end of the workout, I could barely move. My legs, forearms, hands, abdominal muscles, shoulders, biceps, everything hurt. My Polish friends were used to this stuff and it showed; they had a level of fitness, durability, and strength that made them seem like they were constructed in some eastern European laboratory.

It became apparent that this type of exercise helped them be faster, stronger, and more balanced on the job site as well as the soccer field. Jerzy said, "We do this work out because it helps us stay strong. We need it to work because we carry bricks and bags of dirt. We do it for football, too. It makes us feel young!" as he forcefully slapped my back with his chalky and calloused hand. Pawel further explained how common this type of workout was in Eastern Europe for athletes, including footballers, and explained how kettlebells were cheap and mobile and were a staple of athletic conditioning with athletes all over the world.

After the kettlebell workout and calisthenics, I thought the training was over. I was wrong. The group meandered over to the soccer balls and juggled methodically in pairs or threes, and took shots against the north wall trying to hit the duct tape X's off the bounce, or out of the air. After a brief period of soccer warm-ups, we played three-a-side games and passed the time getting thousands of touches on the ball with a series of short, interval passing patterns and possession training. The size of the group oscillated from day-to-day. Some days, the training number swelled to over 20 men and on such days, the odd group out on a drill would run the steel staircases for conditioning.

So, how does this training connect to soccer? Firstly, physical training and soccer performance are interconnected. With that being said, the type of physical training an individual undertakes is critical to the performance on the field. The kettlebell training I took part in does a great deal to improve strength, mobility, and fitness levels. It also improves body control, body composition, and overall physical literacy.

In other words, human anatomy uses three principal planes to transect the body: the sagittal plane, which divides the body into left and right; the coronal plane, which divides the body into dorsal and ventral (back and front, or posterior and anterior) portions; and finally, the transverse plane, which divides the body into superior and inferior (upper and lower) portions in relation to movements.

By performing exercises that stress each plane, an athlete can train and perform more dynamically, especially in a sport like soccer that involves so many types of movements and actions. By engaging high repetition and high-intensity training on the transverse plane, for example, an individual can become a three-dimensional athlete. They can twist, bend, and turn with greater efficiency.

Perhaps the most important benefit of this type of physical training may have very little to do with increasing speed and strength or even power. Instead, it may have more to do with preventing injury and improving body control and balance. This is because training the transverse plane helps prevent injury by strengthening the muscles in the abdominal region that help rotation, power generation, and something called "anti-rotation." Anti-rotation can be viewed as the ability to slow down and control a rotation-based movement (striking a ball, controlling a lofted pass, or performing an aerial movement such as heading the ball or a goalkeeping-based action) after initially generating force through rotation.

Looking back on the experiences with the kettlebell workout and seeing its implementation and popularity increase in the last 20 years, there is some interesting science and psychology behind the high-reps and high-volume training method I did with the Polish team. Dan John is an elite-level strength and weightlifting coach who advocates high-volume Kettlebell training ("10,000 swings in 10 days), and there is further support from the applied physiologist Dr. James Heathers, and the author Matt Perryman ("Squat Every Day").

I want to make it clear that comparing intense physical training made up of high repetitions and volumes is not the same as intense technical training on the ball. What is comparable, however, is the shift in physical capability, mindset hardening, and realization that players can train intensely in a variety of different modalities (physical training or conditioning and technical work, for example).

As the weeks passed, I continued to question why these guys accepted me, but I never asked them. My work ethic and willingness to distribute the pamphlets seemed reason enough. Every Thursday, Jerzy received a notice about a weekend game or two. Other than the job site work, these games were what these men lived and trained for each week. The opponents were often a Latino team, or a local Croatian or Serbian men's team.

Every so often, a pop-up tournament would be announced. These were one-day round-robin format competitions with a pool of money for the winning side. Games were held in warehouses during the winter months and in shoddy parks in the spring and summer. These players had conditioned themselves to a point where they were stronger, more balanced, and had fewer injuries based on their physical training regimen. It proved important for guys who made their living by using their bodies in labor-based jobs.

The games were frenetic and had no referee crews, which meant tempers flared freely. The level of play was faster than anything I played at my current level. It was clear that the city was crawling with players who had played at really high levels in other countries. Having no viable options at the time for professional tiers of the American game, this fraternity of footballers could make more money working as subcontractors while training at the warehouse gym.

In that group, I found a new group of friends. I admired their work ethic and ability to continue training and playing at the highest level they could carve out for themselves. Another lesson they taught was how there was more to being a talented player than ball work, which they certainly did not ignore. Their brand of football was based on strength, speed, and a willingness to work as a unit defensively. I saw first-hand how good these men must have been in their younger years and just how well they maintained their bodies.

For a year, I trained and played in this environment in addition to my club teams. During that time, I would turn out sporadically for a friend's Latino team so long as they were playing in a C.L.A.S.A. (Chicago Latin-American Soccer Association) game, which I knew the Polish team wouldn't play in. By the time I was 18-years-old, my experience, level of fitness, and understanding of the game grew immensely as I was still playing in a top club with players my age and receiving excellent age-appropriate training and match play. But, I also began to unearth playing opportunities that my peers knew nothing about, which I found to be an advantage.

At these hidden levels of the game for the journeyman, there is a gritty yet glamorous pull that keeps players hungry for the sport. Back in my year training in a rusty and dusty warehouse, learning the secrets of how these players – many of them ex-professionals – trained and lived, nothing was complicated, yet everything was done with intensity and purpose. For these men, the high-rep, high-volume training helped them excel and recover from their manual labor jobs, which made them a better team unit on the field.

Looking back, perhaps the most important and interesting aspect of this experience for readers, is how the game exists for those willing to seek it out beyond the conventional constructs of one's sporting shelf-life. In other words, players are conditioned to play throughout their youth and maybe into college before the real world comes calling and forces them to hang up their boots with no viable prospect of playing professionally. These players, however, turned-out for their workouts and matches out of a sense of identity. Working, training, and competing were simply what drove them to continue working towards high levels of physical and soccer-based training. Most of them were extremely talented players with neither the means nor the opportunity to play the game professionally.

Pawel and Jerzy were former professionals in Poland, and they left their country to get jobs in the U.S. They showed their ability time and time again with the way they dominated other teams in the city's Metro League, which housed many former pros and seasoned journeymen.

Perhaps, like many a wishful player, they simply were not good enough for the top levels in Europe and by the time they landed on U.S. shores, they were too old and disconnected to earn a paycheck playing professionally in a country where soccer is not as popular or available as it is abroad. However, in their own version of the game and in their own way, they were gods of the arena.

In autumn of 2003, I was playing for a local university and had been going to the warehouse less frequently to prepare for the collegiate game. I jogged over to the warehouse to find it abandoned. They were gone. I peered through a window and saw that the gym had been hurriedly disassembled.

A Latino man in a pickup truck pulled up and asked me what I was doing there as his work crew brought in kitchen equipment and boxes of tiles to an adjacent building. I asked where the gym was, and he simply said, "No gym here; just the warehouse. The last guys left week, and they stopped paying rent. You know them?" I hesitated before shaking my head unconvincingly.

My year training with these footballing iron men taught me that the game takes on many versions, and happiness in sport often comes down to one's willingness to learn about life through the game – and the game is always there for those who search and work hard enough.

CHAPTER 16: IT TAKES A VILLAGE TO RAISE A PLAYER

Cultural identity and adaptation both foster talent. It is my belief that when an individual can align his or her pursuit with a culture that supports it, they can begin to adapt to the challenges that emerge through progression. There is a fine balance between pushing a player to develop, and pushing a player too far; for most players, that window is only observable in hindsight.

For example, creating a culture of fear can be quite toxic to the development of the person and the player. Players who are ashamed to lose, fear reprimand during the early stages of learning and skill acquisition, and develop under the direction of adults who don't understand the difference between learning and winning, are products of a culture of fear. These players don't want to play; they seek to perform and appease. Over time, they don't learn to express their creativity, which is coached out of them. Eventually, they burn out.

This is why productive modern soccer development models have changed and recognized the difference between a culture that fosters fear, and a culture that fosters exploration. In other words, at the important early stages of player development, top footballing nations have realized that *when winning is removed, development begins.*

So what is a culture of exploration? In terms of player development, it is a system that encourages a variety of learning, training, playing methodologies, environments, and tactics. It also depends on something called improvisation, which is what a player can do with minimal observation, guidance, resources, or external motivation.

Players improve through a variety of approaches. One of those approaches is playing on their own, away from traditional team training settings. Unsupervised and unstructured training and play are immense for a player and social development. However, this type of development does not account for every aspect necessary to produce the type of talent that translates to high-level soccer.

The modern player requires different entry points to address multiple aspects of their development. Traditionally, top players emerge from an environment where the game is part of the social fabric of their society. Today's young player, though, exists in a hyper-organized society that continues to distance individuals from playing opportunities outside of structured team training.

There is, however, a deeper role that the unstructured, organic game accounts for – with regard to producing talent – that can be considered elite.

If the phrase, "It takes a village to raise a child," is true, it may also be true that it takes a village to raise a footballer, too. Early-stage development is crucial to personal development. Children who know who to turn to in times of need, where to go, and what to do within their environments, are much more likely to succeed and open themselves up to further learning opportunities and future growth. Coaches, parents, colleagues, teachers, mentors, and other support systems are critical.

The problem, however, is that society is separated and fragmented in a multitude of extreme ways. Some players will grow up with every need met and every resource available to them at their time of necessity. For others, and probably the vast majority, life will look different. They will have to be searchers and learn through extensive self-exploration, trial and error, failure, and perseverance. The type of player emerging from each environment is drastically different.

So what does this "village" look like when it comes to player development? For each player, it will be different; and for most players, it will not be something quantified in terms of close proximity to where they live. Top players often have to leave where they live to find *their village*, so to speak. Much of this book has been dedicated to the universal truths of a competitive playing journey that can take a player far from home to foreign lands, to obscure places, and which thrusts them into precarious situations. Players who are truly dedicated to reaching their ceiling in the game – wherever that may be – become searchers and masters of improvisation and adaptation.

The Brain Game

Although societal and cultural aspects play a massive role in player development, there is a biological aspect that cannot be overlooked. One of the most important tasks in sport science, and the analysis of performance, is understanding the relationship between skill acquisition (learning the abilities) and the development of talent and excellence (applying and executing *those learned abilities* in meaningful competition on a consistent basis and in a repeatable manner).

The brain is one of the largest and is the most complex organ in the human body. Think of it as the control panel for your life and everything that takes place during your lifespan. It is both the hard drive and the operating system of the human body, and is the data center of the human experience. The brain is made up of more than 100 billion nerves communicating in trillions of connections called synapses. Everything we experience is received, analyzed, and processed through the brain – from the most basic yet crucial aspects of life, such as breathing, sleeping, and heartbeat regulation. However, our brains are complex superhighways of information.

The part of the brain called the amygdala consists of the two almond-shaped groups of cores located deep and medially within the temporal lobes of the brain. This area controls the limbic system, which controls memory, decision-making, and emotional responses. Additionally, in this area of the brain lies how we access our long-term memory. People gain experience by using the limbic system's power to log information, processes, and procedures largely through repetition and trial-and-error experiences. These experiences are registered and eventually reinforced through episodes consisting of a single action, the input, and its associated result – the output. This output, or result of each input action, is generally categorized as a reward or a consequence. Now, imagine countless sequences, just like this, repeatedly occurring during a lifespan. Such sequences form a pattern that reinforces habit and helps shape future behavior.

Here's a simple example to help paint the picture. We've heard of the hot stove scenario in which a child has no prior experience of what "hot" is, let alone what it feels like. In fact, the entire experience is unknown because it has not happened yet and, therefore, has not been processed, logged, and analyzed by the brain. This child only learns that the stove is hot through direct interaction with the scorching surface. Although this child can be told that the stove is hot, and warned about the consequences through direct verbal instruction, without that prior experience and the associated sensations to that experience, little value is derived from the verbal instruction – the warning. And so, the child touches the stove, and determinative pain signals are seared into their body, brain, and behavior regulation system in an instant.

As we develop, the brain functions like a computer's scanning function, looking for patterns of past incidents and experiences that are attempted to send the appropriate response. And, like a computer system scanning the hard drive, and the software installed on it, the scans become more efficient and quicker as patterns are grouped systematically. This is called experience. But there is something more creative about acquiring experience related to skill acquisition.

People are generally quick learners and will continue to amass experiences largely through repetition and trial-and-error, especially towards specific tasks and pursuits. In the context of this book, skill development in soccer relies heavily on these formative experiences and their associated feeling.

Obviously, though, we need to move beyond the hot stove scenario.

Consider the sensation of pain from a kick or a fall, or the euphoria from scoring, or the anxiety and fear during bouts of competition, or channeling basic levels of confidence – these are processes of the limbic system triggering responses linked to habit formation.

In the realm of sport, the same emotional and physical conditions can trigger responses that also improve performance by augmenting the right combination of feelings and commands that the brain feels are necessary. In a way, this is how habits are formed that can be scanned and accessed or retrieved on the pitch. Within the context of sport, individuals experiencing anxiety are likely to access a familiar pattern of events and behaviors that resulted in unfavorable consequences, and so the amygdala sends the appropriate signals to handle the situation.

To help apply this to a scenario, let's return to the example involving the hot stove. A child is told the stove is hot, but the child doesn't understand what "hot" feels like, so they touch it. That resulting pain pattern is logged, and the child gains an experiential "dataset" that is imprinted and stored for future retrieval.

Applying this basic understanding to sport is crucial. The more often an individual performs a task, the more neurological pathways are formed. These pathways are ensconced in what is called myelin, which is a combination of protein material and phospholipids that wrap around the nerves in the brain and spinal cord, and which allow electrical impulses to be transmitted efficiently.

In life, people develop ability through repetition assigned to specific tasks over time. In soccer, for example, a player dedicating extensive focus and time performing specific tasks will form stronger myelin connections that link the *feeling* and *decision-making* associated with that skill while storing the necessary procedures for successful task completion in their short-term memory. Such a process has both positive and negative results related to performance. Development takes time and repetition towards a specific skill-based task. The challenge becomes learning to stack more effective habit-formation patterns *rather than* reinforcing bad habit patterns.

At a certain age, the focus of high-level players shifts as they develop a serious passion or obsession for improvement and progression. Again, this is different for each individual, and there are several factors that can either turn this shift into an overall positive part of their development or a major impediment. Without proper guidance, and that "village" to help steer them in the right direction, players on a competitive track often hone their entire focus on what *they can control* and dedicate themselves wholly to the tasks set before them. These tasks might include producing a specific technique or skill at the direction of a coach, or an impulse from their own observation.

Comparing the psychology of players who grew up with free play versus those from predominately organized and supervised settings can help explain how a player develops. Those with more playing experiences outside of formal training learn how to deal with the emotions associated with a performance largely on their own. Players tend to gain experience through a cause and effect approach without a coach-based prompt or instruction for much of their upbringing. This is where experimenting and improvisation are uniquely developed. Players are free to make their own decisions and experience the gamut of possible outcomes, which is critical in so many aspects of not only sport, but life.

On the other side of the spectrum, players with a formative upbringing in organized settings are conditioned to play with reward-based directives coming from a coach or parent. This type of formative learning can uniquely affect personal, social, and sporting development by conditioning the ability to process, understand, synthesize, and apply direct instruction towards a prescribed learning objective or outcome. In this setting, players can begin to understand the value of process and procedure, which are necessary components in learning, working in a team environment, and operating well within a tactical set-up.

It should be noted that both types of development – free play and organized play – are necessary to help improve a player's ability in sport and even socially over time. Both settings develop and test intelligence models for players. The modern debates around coaching topics often relegate fundamental aspects to being *one or the other* scenarios, which over-simplifies and obfuscates rather complex developmental conditions.

Evolution through Observation

A concept like getting thousands of touches on the ball a day remains an open-ended evolution of conventional player development axioms. It is constantly open to interpretation, adaptation, and further modification.

For example, look at a typical youth practice. At the beginning of the session, some kids stand and talk, and others grab a ball and shoot at an empty goal. But every so often, there will be some kids who naturally work on their game in a multitude of ways. Some play keep away in small groups. Others dribble past stationary and distracted buddies, triggering 1-on-1 duels of creativity and focused technique training. At many training sessions, you can look at a practice and, within five minutes, you can tell who the *players* are – the ones working on "moves" in isolation or together – while other kids stand around and others take pot shots.

Growing up, the game was part of life. As odd as that may sound for someone growing up in the United States in the mid-1980s, and through the 1990s, it was all down to my environment and willingness to find the game. In those early years, we just had *fun* and played for the *fun* of it. It was my father who first noticed how many times we would touch the ball. Some players would have to wait for rides, and it could take quite a while to be picked up (this being before cell phones were commonplace), but we would continue to play with the ball. As players advance and move from team to team, and through the levels of the game, they must incorporate what they've learned and honed as skills into their daily practice – even at the expense of results.

Another aspect of that "village" a player needs to develop is the core of five or six players who advance and develop with them on a given team or within a community; players who are pretty good that stay and play together over the years. The evolution is often quick and obvious; after a few seasons, kids become real players. The kids who excel are often the ones who keep up their own training on the ball without instruction and prompting. For them, it's natural and innate. There is no counting, just a sense of wanting to improve as individuals and as a core.

Such conditions allow players to relish competition in a healthy way because they can form internal competitions and develop a sharper skillset. Going back to my own days as a young player, that core group of players was always present on every good team I played on. The players and teams might have changed over the years, but the key was finding a way to be part of the core group that spoke a common footballing language around forming and fostering a relationship with the ball. Doing so allowed me to find people with similar values to those I possessed, which helped forge lasting friendships. Even outside of formal practice, we always had a ball around – not necessarily to directly "train" but as a fundamental and central piece of our *identity* as players.

CHAPTER 17: THE COACHING CONUNDRUM

The role of coach for a young team that is just beginning its journey in the game is a crucial appointment. For most young teams, the role of coach and team manager generally falls on a parent or someone working as a volunteer. Such a position is important in the development of each young player in social, emotional, and technical/tactical senses.

In the early stages, the game is simple, and the role of the coach is generally to facilitate a social outlet for children while providing a baseline level of structure while teaching basic skills and allowing the players the chance to play. These first experiences in the game, and in a team setting, are incredibly significant for interactions with others and sporting development, and most of the role that a coach adopts often mimics basic principles of parenting; much more so than principles of play.

For example, my mother was my first coach in the game. Like my father, she drew from her experiences as an accomplished athlete in other sports to help guide her journey with a rambunctious group of four- and five-year-old boys clad in blue kits to match our team name, *The Blue Angels* (the inspiration being the United States Navy flight demonstration squadron).

However, the role of the volunteer parent-coach is often limited to instructing players on where to stand, how to listen and absorb direct instruction, and a myriad of other compliance-based traits that are inherently important. In turn, from the onset – depending on the competitiveness and ability of the team and its players – much of the time is devoted to skills that can take away from actually playing the game. At those young ages, I believe that young players should be allowed to explore, experiment, and express themselves freely. More often than not, practice time for four- and five-year-old kids is about social interaction and having a safe environment to play, run around, and develop connections with their peers.

Growing up in Northern California's Bay Area near Moffett Federal Airfield, a joint civil-military air command and airport facility located in unincorporated Santa Clara, the sight of fighter jets and military cargo and reconnaissance aircraft was common. This is important because one of the ways my mother – with no history in the game – encouraged a young group of boys to "buy-in" to her coaching as a team was to let us pick the team name. We kicked a ball around and chased one another when all of a sudden, a squadron of dark blue jets screamed by overhead. Startled, we looked upward to see the aircraft negotiating high velocity and difficult maneuvers.

With our heads craned to the sky, I remember the collective excitement of naming our team after those jets. My mother told us to think of the Blue Angels when we took to the field to practice. She asked us to play fast on the attack and stick together in a formation on defense – not a bad bit of coaching from a volunteer wrangling a bunch of boys on a field a few times a week. Although she was a wonderful role model and dedicated her time to ensuring our betterment as a team, she could only do so much based on her knowledge of the game. Again, her role was not to develop players. Her role was to organize the practice and games schedule and supervise young players while *maybe* teaching us a thing or two about the sport.

That first year in the game is pure. Ideally, it is less about scoring goals, learning skills, and wins and losses, and more about the experience of learning something new. I suppose that is the beauty of youth sports at their best. Inevitably, however, that journey changes for every player. It soon becomes apparent that the landscape of the youth game points players in two distinct, yet contrasting, directions: competitive or recreational.

When you're young, these words mean very little, but it doesn't take long to figure out the difference between the two routes. That first team I played on was quite good – at least in terms of being able to keep the ball and enjoy the sport, since we all grew up playing the game in a culture that fostered it. And so, we all chose the competitive route. I was just happy my teammates all decided to stick together for another season.

This presents a potential conundrum with regards to coaching at the youngest levels during the more formative and introductory years; players may spend *several years* being coached by volunteers whose knowledge is limited. This entire topic is really a piece of a much larger and complex puzzle regarding the governance and oversight of the game from a federation or association level. For example, in the last 20 years, Iceland has totally revamped its footballing culture, coaching education, and best practices, in an effort to continue to produce capable footballers who can go abroad and succeed. In order to do so, Iceland did what most other countries simply cannot do regarding its coaching appointments at the youth levels by appointing UEFA-qualified coaches at the young levels for all players. Obviously, the size and population of the country – along with its sporting resources and training sites – make it a unique case to study, but there are elements of its model that are worth exploring and applying elsewhere.

The Icelandic Model

In 2015, I spoke to Arnar Bill Gunnarsson who, at the time, was the Director of Education for the Icelandic Football Association (KSÍ) for *These Football Times*. Gunnarsson believed Icelandic football's improvement was the result of the KSÍ delivering consistency in its governance of the game: a quality coaching education program paired with the advantages of a smaller island population.

Gunnarsson, who holds a UEFA A coaching license, discussed the systematic approach Iceland took to build on the achievements of its past footballing exports such as Eidur Gudjohnsen, Gylfi Sigurdsson, Hermann Hreidarsson, Kolbeinn Sigthórsson, and Aron Einar Gunnarsson, while continuing to usher in the success of the present, to forge the road ahead for Icelandic football.

"Football is by far the biggest sport in Iceland. There are about 20,000 players. Players that play games with club teams are the only players we register. We don't count the players who are just playing for fun," he explained.

Regarding the topic of the coaching role at the youngest levels, Iceland's model is perhaps the key reason the standard of football in the country has risen dramatically, rooted as it is in the level of baseline coaching education. For example, in the United States and many other countries, issues such as a pay-to-play model combined with inconsistent and expensive coaching education prices out potential coaches. These issues create a wide chasm and a fragmented educational standard of coaches within the system.

So what is the solution? In countries like Iceland (plus Germany, Spain, Italy, and the Netherlands), coaching is seen as a skilled position. These countries have subscribed to a different way of thinking about coaching education and the qualifications a coach must attain. And the biggest benefactors are the young players; from the start of their footballing journey, they have the immense benefit of getting exposure to highly qualified, paid coaches. This practice helps produce players with a strong technical and foundational base and a coachable, team-centric mentality.

Gunnarsson highlighted the importance and impact of appointing qualified and licensed coaches to the youngest age groups. "The key is when the players start training at four or five years of age, they get a qualified, paid coach. Almost every coach in Iceland has a coaching qualification. They have a UEFA B or UEFA A license. So when you are a four- or five- or even three-year-old, you get a qualified and experienced coach.

"If kids get an experienced and qualified coach who is fun and entertaining, the kids love the game. What happens when you learn to love the game, you go out on the training pitch and do something extra. You play football outside of organized training sessions. That is the mentality in Iceland. If you look at the other Scandinavian countries – Norway, Denmark, Sweden – in most cases, there are parents coaching the kids until they are 12-years-old, as volunteers."

It's one thing to look at Iceland's model and draw direct comparisons, but things get more complex when conceptualized and applied elsewhere. Iceland has a distinct advantage due to its smaller landmass and population density – factors that for many countries would prove to be hindrances. Although the commitment to a higher standard of coaching education works well for Iceland's population size, it's yet to be accomplished in a country like the United States with a massive population and landmass and a disjointed federation. Additionally, there is great value in having parents and volunteers who truly want to learn about the game serving in coaching roles at the earliest ages. That way, they can learn how the game is played and taught and can better understand what their son or daughter is experiencing.

Back in Iceland, Gunnarsson argued that the absence of volunteer coaches produces a higher pedigree of player. "If you compare that concept with a qualified, paid coach in Iceland who has gone through all the courses through the Icelandic FA with a parent in Norway or Sweden, it's a win-win situation in Iceland.

"That is why we are able to produce so many good players even though we are so few. Twenty years ago, we didn't do it regularly, so we didn't qualify, but we are getting better. It's not something that happened suddenly."

My Father, My Coach

Growing up with a mother doing her best to serve as a volunteer coach for my first year in the game remains a special memory and experience for me. At some point, however, we decided to take the competitive route as a team. There was then the problem of finding enough teams at our age at the appropriate competitive level, so we played three years up. We also didn't have a coach when my mother had to take on a new role at work. Additionally, no fathers could spare time to volunteer to coach us in a league where we would certainly be demolished week after week.

And so, my father stepped up to coach us. It was awkward with him as my coach. I'd only known him as Dad. The first lesson he taught me was that I would be treated like everyone else – there would be no special treatment. That was a lie. He was harder on me than the others, and I often was put at odds with his disciplinary actions. When a group was made to run extra sprints or pick up the gear after losing a game, I joined in regardless of my involvement.

This was all by design; something I would come to realize years later. My father dedicated his life to helping others. His drive was to help others see in themselves the potential he saw. Although he never played soccer at a high level, he played enough high-level sports and dedicated much of his life to the process of improving and expanding his skill set to apply what he learned to the development of players he coached. I was fortunate to have him coach me during my formative years. The following coaching and developmental principles he showcased remain relevant almost 30 years later.

My father framed his coaching approach as a "Process versus Execution" principle when he took over. To make up for his lack of experience playing the game, he constantly studied what top coaches abroad believed, and would spend countless hours reading and watching films of foreign leagues at the library. He forced himself to become a student of the game – he did all of this so he could better coach a youth team.

Years later, he admitted that he rarely saw a player who was committed to being a student of the game, but the ones he did see commit themselves to the process went far in the game. He wanted to show us that there is more than one way to watch a game, and most only watch for entertainment. Another relatable concept that current coaches could begin to teach their players is a lesson he taught me and anyone willing to learn – *how to truly watch a game.*

"Kids who would try and watch soccer and go to a game with a willingness to learn went furthest. Anyone would watch the World Cup, but very few would watch the game with an intent to learn the game," he recalled. "Students of the game are willing to take what they see on TV, emulate it, and strive to improve upon it. Mere mimicking of what you see isn't good enough."

He stressed the need for us to study the game in such a way that we could learn how to play the game in many different and abstract ways. Obviously, this required more than merely sitting and watching the game. It required watching the formations and seeing how they shifted and adjusted to the game conditions. On the occasion I could attend matches in-person, I made it a point to walk down to the field for the team warm-up. I was mesmerized watching the off-the-ball runs, movements, and routines of the players. There, I could see how so much of the game was played off-the-ball. The real treat was listening to the players in real-time as they played.

Principles of Play

"Fail to prepare, prepare to fail." We heard that phrase almost every session, and my father did not shy away from a chance to remind us what it really meant. From my earliest years preparing to play, the need to train, compete, and *learn* was a non-negotiable aspect of being on competitive teams.

My father and many of my best coaches all stressed this principle in nuanced yet similar ways. One example that was common at every high-level team I played on was an unwritten rule about shooting before training. At no time were we allowed to shoot on an empty goal before warming up, even if nobody was at the field yet. Shooting blindly and wildly at an empty goal before properly warming up is both unwise and unrealistic. It is also a time-wasting activity since we seldom hit the back of the net; instead, we found the parking lot to be a more consistent landing place for our errant shots.

Once my father took over coaching my team, we played three years up in the league divisions. He focused on preparing us to play by implementing more preparation-based steps before training and games. This phase seemed like overkill, and felt laborious, but one of the costs of playing up several years was fine-tuning our pre-game rituals and disciplines. When other teams in our youth league gathered around the goal or the 18-yard box and lined up to shoot (often missing the goal) before a game, my father watched. Sometimes, he observed with a pen in hand as he tallied the balls that soared over the goal or well-wide of the mark.

"Look at their body language. Look at how they don't care if they miss the target. They think this is a joke," he'd say before reinforcing his points with a follow-up. "Don't look at the shot; look at the run-up and then their reaction. Watch how long it takes them to go get their balls and come back to the box. What a waste of time."

Even with his limited knowledge of the game, my father knew it was obvious that nobody thought about *why* they missed or *how* they missed so often. However, he wanted us to take notice as we prepared to play, even if it was just for a minute or two. We began to see these other players not only as older, stronger, and faster players. We saw them as players who did not take pride in their preparation. We noticed they had limited knowledge or desire to correct their mistakes. The same players would miss shot after shot for an entire pre-game warm-up. The profound aspect of this principle was that it gave us a steely and silent confidence. We weren't watching the opponent take shots; we were watching an activity of blindly kicking the ball!

The next principle he focused on was application. During our preparation phase, we observed the other team and reframed our perspective. This was something that was necessary, given the age difference. As a coach, he wanted us to win on the field, but to do so, we needed to learn and gain some moral victories, too.

While the pre-match, pot-shot routine resembled a team practicing insanity, we practiced differently. Our focus was to apply that which we observed as we prepared. While *they* were getting marginally better by dumb luck (hitting the target once in a while off a pre-match shot), *we* focused on improving by focusing on fundamental skills and activities once we arrived at the field. Back then, teams rarely worked to improve their technique beyond the foundational skills – that responsibility fell on the player.

"I tried to do what I thought of as weird and stupid things," Dad recalled. "I needed to experiment with creative ways to help us improve."

One notable example was when he tried to get players to use their less dominant foot. He brought a bag of old socks out and made each player put a sock on their dominant foot. The set-up made us find a way to touch the ball and play with our less dominant foot, so we weren't as reliant on our strong foot.

Another thing parents initially considered a "stupid thing" was dribble patterns in training. He lined us up on one of the penalty areas and started a stopwatch. At the whistle, he instructed us to dribble at pace but under control getting one-touch on the ball per step while avoiding the other players in a condensed space (while not relying on our dominant foot, since we all wore those socks upon arrival). The genius of it was that there was no set pattern for us to dribble, nor was there a prescribed set of moves or feints he demanded of us. Of course, setting out lines of countless cones and predetermined grids would have been the more conventional and orthodox way of setting up training, but he wanted us to dribble naturally. His learning objective was to allow us to find a way through the mess of players dribbling around, which required us to slow down, pick our heads up, use all surfaces of both feet, and a variety of dribbling techniques.

The really contentious part of his coaching was in games. For a man who didn't grow up playing the game, he had a unique footballing philosophy that would likely align with progressive coaching methods today. One stipulation was the "ten-pass rule". If we were not circulating the ball enough, he would insist that we had to pass the ball ten times before anyone could take a shot, regardless of what the score was or the importance of the game.

Obviously, this framed the game in a different lens for us because it took our attention away from individualistic and exhibitionist priorities, and instilled in us a team-based collective possession philosophy and style of play, instead. The parents, however, did not buy-in to this *whatsoever*. They wanted Route One play and goals. The more they demanded kick-and-run play, the more he refused to budge because, at our age, the game was still about learning how to play as a collective and dominate the ball. The irony of it all – which parents did not understand – was that our win rate was higher when we implemented the "ten-pass rule" than when we tried to bomb the ball forward and make it a kick-and-chase affair against teams that were bigger, faster, and stronger than us.

Winning versus Developing

Growing up, I was fortunate to play for coaches who realized the outcome of the game should matter, but not as much as how the game was played. Most of my coaches knew that the development of skills, and understanding of how to play, mattered more than the score. The brutal truth is many young players don't know when to run, how to run, or where to run off the ball. They are reactive players. Like most technically and tactically deficient players, they are just doing what they were taught. The whole game is more of an exercise in *doing* rather than *thinking*.

If we look back at the late-1970s through the early-1990s, there were generations of players who were seemingly told not to cross the halfway line, or that defenders only defend by blasting the ball into the stands or up the field, or that attacking players can't defend from the front. The startling way that ignorance breeds ignorance epitomized the game for years and, in many ways, still does. During that same time in the United States, for example, soccer became a high-cost suburban sport, and socially what mattered was winning over development as families and participants wanted a return on investment for each season. This ushered in the pay-to-play business model that continues to define the game in the United States.

I remember talking to Terry Michler one day in his classroom in St. Louis, and he recalled his youth playing in what was known as the Pepsi League and what the system was like in the parochial school and parish set-up. I wanted to know what that culture was like and how it fostered the game and developed players in the U.S. in ways that may be missing today.

Regarding the parochial school and parish set-up, Michler revealed a cultural aspect that is more aligned with the game abroad, which existed before it shifted to its current business-driven model.

"Soccer was very big in the Catholic school system when I was young (a la 1950s, 1960s). Every school had soccer teams, and the competition between neighboring schools was always intense. There were City Championships in all the age groups and that gave you big-time bragging rights. You also had rivalries between North and South St. Louis schools and the more established schools wanted to test 'their mettle' against the rest of the best. It was a very healthy competition, regulated by the CYC (Catholic Youth Council) with their laws and by-laws."

The impact of the community-based culture of St. Louis soccer extended well beyond the youth levels, which helped inspire entire generations of players and teams to develop and represent the city.

"At the senior level, there was an annual CYC All-Star game where our local senior CYC All-Stars would play a top European club. Over the years, clubs came from all over: Canada, Mexico, England, Chile, Germany, Brazil, Czechoslovakia, Sweden, Scotland, France and Turkey, among others. Manchester United came twice, in 1950 and 1960, and Manchester City in 1958, playing matches at the Public Schools Stadium – a field dedicated in 1928 to fulfilling a long-standing city need for a centralized location for hosting school-based athletics competitions. The St. Louis teams almost always lost, though there was a 1-1 tie with Liverpool in 1964."

Terry Michler then addressed a unique league in St. Louis. "The Pepsi League was formed in the 1960s with Pepsi Cola being the sole sponsor for the eight-team league. Pepsi Cola was big into soccer sponsorship as they did a series of training films featuring Pelé that were actually shot in Brazil. Pepsi even brought Pelé to the USA to do appearances and clinics.

"The eight teams represented the St. Louis region – north, south, and central – each team was appointed a coach who would then select players of his choice from within the geographical boundaries of his assigned area. This was truly a Select situation – players were selected by the manager, no cost to play, equipment (personal gear) provided free of charge, and quality competition. The League continued into the 70s and then clubs began to take over the soccer scene and pay-to-play became the norm. Select soccer became "collect soccer" – you play, you pay, we collect."

The youth game is a tumultuous landscape of feeder clubs and what we will call super clubs. Depending on the geography, these super clubs are more prestigious and popular as they have the resources, labels, connections, and funding to take upwards of 70% of the top talent in a given area. The reality for these larger clubs – especially during my upbringing – was that they could beat everyone, but they rarely developed anyone.

At the time, as is the case now, these clubs had 11 players that had been developed elsewhere, playing against teams where maybe six or seven truly talented players had not yet been siphoned into the super club system. The system is often structured around results over all else, and the super clubs will often win everything in sight.

So what's the point?

At a particular stage in a player's journey, the game is firmly about results and – to achieve success and recognition – players have to play for teams that win. The problem, however, is some teams are never about development, but about acquiring talent.

Going back to my own upbringing, my father was aware of the system's set-up, and it was never his intention to defeat or defy the reality of the youth soccer landscape in the United States. His ultimate goal was about winning through player development, which is antithetical to many of the practices that take place in the competitive youth soccer ecosystem.

When I asked about the emergence of the superclub in the youth game, my father said, "They didn't care about player development. They cared about winning. They wanted hardware. Not hard results or hard players. When their players went to higher levels, the players didn't succeed because they didn't have players who could actually compete. That's what happens when you form super teams that aren't tested often because they have eliminated the competition. Winning doesn't always mean quality. It means winning. It doesn't always equate or isn't conducive to developing players. It means putting the best players on the field regardless of who developed them."

And so it remains in the modern game.

CHAPTER 18: THE ART OF SWEATING THE SMALL STUFF

When I began writing this book, I had to learn many things. One of the biggest lessons was homing in on the details and microprocesses that make up the bigger picture. One such lesson was delving deeper into the aspects of specificity of this "simple game" and examining the importance of attention to detail. It's no secret that doing the little things well is a skill, and if a player can form good habits early on, they can hopefully begin to find new levels, abilities, and approaches that will likely extend beyond the pitch and into their lives.

One dominant memory of mine is when I was quite young after losing a game to an older and more superior team. On the drive home after the game, my sweat-soaked red Umbro uniform still clings to my body, and my grass-stained socks are rolled down low. My black and red Mitre boots (that I hastily kicked off) are on the floorboard, still tied, and my feet are jammed into a pair of scuffed white Reebok Classic trainers.

On my face is a scowl that I see in the side-view mirror.

I had been playing organized soccer for about four or five years, and this was the first season of truly competitive play several levels higher than I was accustomed to playing. This bump up in age-level competition and standard of play had a unique effect on my development, and perception of the game in positive and negative ways.

This may seem uncommon today, but playing different ages was part of sporting experiences growing up, whether it was scrimmaging another team or playing pick-up games.

Anyway, we had lost 6-1.

I remember not necessarily caring about the final score. Like my teammates, I was relieved when the final whistle blew – or at least I thought I was. Then, something happened when a teammate's father said, "It's fine, guys. Who cares about the score...don't sweat the small stuff."

For some reason, that line didn't just irritate me, it set me off. Perhaps I was looking for someone to blame or a place to target my dissatisfaction. Young people, as I have learned as a coach and as a father, tend to do this from time-to-time. But, for some reason, my immaturity pushed me over the edge. I was incensed.

The entire ride home, my father tried to distract me from the result. The truth was, I couldn't care less about losing. It was the *manner* in which we lost that bothered me. I was more introspective than my teammates to a fault, and I didn't know what to expect at that level. A familiar game had suddenly become unfamiliar.

Honestly, I still have no idea what I expected. What should have happened did happen. Superior players and a better-developed team beat us in every aspect of the game. The thing about losing in anything is we seldom allow ourselves to extract the teachable moment, or learn the lesson, because emotions take control of our attitudes and actions.

Tethered to my ire was the line: "Don't sweat the small stuff."

After rebuking my father's attempts to change the mood by going fishing (he always had our fishing poles and tackle boxes in the back of the pickup truck), or to go get lunch, he finally sighed and asked me what I wanted to do.

"I want to go play. Right now."

I didn't think he heard me, but he pulled off at the next exit and motored towards a nearby park.

My eyes met my father's, and he nodded.

I thought he was calling my bluff. But I was serious. I wanted to work on something. Even though I didn't know how to articulate it at the time, the truth was that there had to be catharsis.

Building the Routine

I grabbed my ball and pulled the door handle and stepped out of the truck. Underfoot, the concrete parking lot was smooth and flat, yet strewn with random cracks complete with weeds and grass jutting out here and there.

My father walked over and told me to dribble and use the cracks, parking lot lines, and debris as indicators to perform a move, turn, or change of pace. Before I began, he said, "Have fun out there. Just play."

Obviously, it's easier to dribble against shadows instead of actual opponents, but this wasn't about competing with anyone else. It was about turning a negative into a positive action. Before long, my father was using his Timex Ironman watch timer to prescribe times for me to dribble at pace. After a few 30-second bouts, this turned into an informal yet extremely fun training session.

My father's approach was simple and effective. Instead of catering to my pouting and allowing me to harbor a petulant and negative attitude, he allowed me to go out and put that energy to work.

He also knew that if I had the energy to complain, I had the energy to apply myself towards some kind of physical outlet. The best part was this wasn't a punishment. He didn't dwell on the loss. He just knew I was conflicted.

In that moment, however, something remarkable happened.

I was sweating the small stuff. In fact, I was pouring sweat. And it was invigorating and liberating.

The following week, we won our first game. My attitude was obviously better, but a routine was established. We returned to the parking lot for more dribbling practice, which soon turned into dribbling patterns mixed with striking the ball against a brick wall and passing it against parking lot curbs to practice taking the ball out of the air before continuing my dribbling. Soon, a few teammates that carpooled with us joined in, and we looked forward to the detour to play 1-on-1 or 2-on-2 games on the way home.

Over the next few weeks, I looked forward to spending time playing in that cracked concrete parking lot with my father just as much as I looked forward to playing in the games, which we continued to struggle in and lose more than we won. I began to stop obsessing over unrealistic outcomes and began to enjoy the game more. I learned that it was a privilege to play against older and superior players and to get an idea of what the game not only looked like at the next level – but to experience what it felt and played like there, too.

Perhaps it all was borne out of petulance and negativity. But, through those elements, I extracted a valuable lesson. We often focus on the aggregate of events, which can make it difficult to learn from if we don't shift our focus to the things we can control; things that play a part in the larger picture. For me, it was playing a game, often losing, and then immediately figuring out a way to focus on one or two aspects of my play that I could work on with a renewed perspective.

Attention to Detail

Here's what I have learned in my playing, training, coaching, studying, and writing about the game for most of my life. For the driven, competitive player, the small stuff is precisely what an individual should sweat — be it perfecting a move or technique, honing and improving fitness, or studying and applying some mental endurance. A player on a competitive journey needs to pour themselves into a process or series of processes that are geared to push their abilities.

Focusing on attention to detail (a better way of "sweating the small stuff") is one area everyone can improve in almost immediately.

Attention to detail is often task-driven and pertains to an individual's ability to efficiently allocate their intellectual resources to achieve a higher level of thoroughness and accuracy when accomplishing an undertaking. With regards to sport, these perceptive skills allow players to improve their training habits, productivity during sessions, decision-making efficiency, and performance during meaningful competition.

Top players make quality a priority and develop focused routines that allow them to address their weaknesses in a variety of scenarios, and improve them through simulation-based exercises. It also enables and teaches players to be present and to manage "the moment" in the pursuit of that specific task. This being said, players don't just develop this attention to detail at the required levels. Coaches play a unique role in developing this quality in a player's profile.

Several years ago, I had the pleasure of working with Tim Lees, who has coached at Wigan, Watford, Liverpool, and the United States Development Academy. Over the years, Tim has learned from the likes of Roberto Martinez, Brendan Rodgers, and Pep Lijnders, to name a few. Tim is one of the best coaches I've worked with, and one of the most progressive and educated coaches and voices in the game today.

During our time coaching together, and seeing his work since, the approach Tim Lees uses is a blueprint for complete individual player development. His model is predicated on allowing players to express themselves but also to play to their specific strengths. To do so, players need to understand the details of their *own* style and train accordingly. This doesn't mean they cannot learn new skills or develop more aspects to their games. It means they must learn to sharpen their skillsets and gain a better understanding of not only who they are as players, but who they want to be and who they should emulate. Tim effectively explained the role of a coach in developing players and fostering their unique skillsets.

"Every young player has a unique skillset and profile. Whatever their identity and strength(s) are at a young age; always the same strength a decade later. The coach's job is to make them *more* of what they are... enhance strengths whilst making sure weaknesses aren't enough to be exposed."

Tim has also stated the importance of detailed and focused individual work to develop position-specific, dominant one-on-one specialists, which requires a high level of attention to detail. "If sessions for individual players are the same, then there is no focus on individual development. Positional exercises merely dive into the top layer. Each player has specific strengths within the position, and should focus on replicating prioritized scenarios to bring those out."

Attention to detail is important, but don't get it confused with obsessing over failure and over-analyzing every situation. Establishing a solid training and mental routine also puts forth a process that helps a player develop their own developmental framework. But is there such thing as too much attention to detail? In short, yes, there is. By devoting time and effort towards a specific skill or task, all the energy and focus is directed towards the preparation, performance, and completion of that task.

But too much direction and instruction at the wrong levels, and with incorrect context, can prove detrimental. Young players can focus on manageable chunks of information to process and perform for so long before they grow tired of a routine or direct instruction. In the hyper-organized industry of academy football, there remains a risk of developing players that know every tactical formation and set-up they've been taught, but when it comes to the one-on-one aspect of the game, they struggle.

This was evident in 2018, when German football hit another low point after once again reaching the pinnacle of the world's game. For the first time in history, the German national team crashed out in the group stage of the FIFA World Cup and was then eliminated from the UEFA Nations League.

An article that same year in Forbes, by football writer Manuel Veth, shed light on a reality that German football experienced. "There is also a deeper fundamental problem. Bundesliga teams are no longer German youth football factories. In fact, the current wave of young talent is mostly driven by young English, French and Eastern European talent seeking to make their next steps in their careers."

German football had become a victim of the very thing that made it the dominant force – hyper-organization and tactical discipline. These foundational pillars of play seemed to turn out more drone-like robotic players than creators on the pitch.

The article added, "All of this highlights the biggest problem that German football faces at the moment. Young international players have abilities that cannot be found among young German players."

Oliver Bierhoff, a former national team striker and national team sporting director, told the German media, "When clubs prefer to sign young English, French or Belgian players, then there is only one solution. Young German players have to get better."

This directly relates to a situation where too much attention to detail may play a role. In the article, Bierhoff identified that young German players struggle with one-on-one situations and no longer have what Germans call *Bolzplatzmentalität* – a football identity developed away from organized football.

Like Germany, soccer is often over-theorized. Top youth players, especially at the youngest ages where the coaching is most formative, are often perfectly able to understand tactical set-ups and deployment schemes based on match situations. Where they struggle is when the game breaks down into individual duels. It is here that players who have learned to play in the streets, cages, and on the courts for countless hours have a distinct advantage and who can often unlock even the most rigidly disciplined teams tactically.

The modern game has never been more tactically advanced or fluid. Training models and methods are often rehearsed to the point of perfection. That being said, the need for the creative player, or as Tim Lees calls it, "the Maverick" has never been more apparent. This player can be developed in a variety of ways; however, the most important aspects are centered around ball mastery with game-realistic and position-specific movements (turns, feints, cuts, chops, rolls, etc.) Eventually, players can be developed who can make decisions to outplay others in intense one-on-one scenarios, at any point, with confidence.

A Portuguese Perspective

In 2003, when José Mourinho's FC Porto began ushering in an era of success in both Portuguese and European football, his assistant manager, Rui Faria, said, "What happens is that the ultimate goal is to play. And if this is to be achieved, training can have only one meaning: do it by playing. If the aim is to improve the quality of play and organization, these parameters can only be implemented through training situations or exercises where you can work this organization. Given this, only through a specific exercise, you can manage these objectives."

I found in studying and attending numerous presentations of *Tactical Periodization* that one of José Mourinho's main coaching philosophies is the idea that players absorb the ideas and concepts of the coach through

168

the systematic repetition of certain exercises and drills during training over the course of a season (or several seasons).[25]

These ideas, values, and concepts are drip-fed into the team's collective philosophy over time. This is why an accepted truth in management and development reinforces Mourinho's approach; soccer is a sport requiring a cohesive training plan that progressively builds up to levels that are increasingly rigorous, and which meet the actual game-based needs of the competition.

In this context, the planning and approach for a team or even a player should be viewed as the actual structuring and organization of preparation of programs *for actual competition*. As such, players will be exposed to training situations and schemes that vary in complexity and intensity as required by the demands of the level at which they play.

Because soccer is a sport that requires players to have a sense of what specificity means – in relation to their skillset and ability, plus the team's collective needs – coaches like Mourinho have put great emphasis on this relationship in terms of the psycho-cognitive, physical, and tactical aspects of the game. In essence, the coach's job is to solve the puzzle, and the players are the pieces of that puzzle.

The Principle of Specificity

The role of specificity is a reinforcing principle regarding the specialization of training towards a targeted activity or sport. In other words, the principle of specificity suggests that training should be relevant, appropriate, and focused on the sport for which an individual is training in order to produce the desired performance effect. Furthermore, sport-specific training should be progressive – with a trajectory starting at general conditioning to particular instruction and training for the precise skills and tasks required in that sport.

With regards to soccer, specificity should be thought of as the observable and traceable relationship between all relevant dimensions of a match and the training associated with the preparation for meaningful competition. Returning to Mourinho's coaching philosophy, the training exercises are precisely representative of the team's model of play. The

---

[25] I must credit the coaching community for making the opportunity and availability of these resources open to so many studying development.

result is the theory related to the principle of specificity drives and directs the training process over time.

It is best to recognize the relationship between the overall game model and the specific principles related to the game model on an individualized level as something hierarchical. That is, players and coaches should be able to identify a playing style's principles (core competencies) that drive sub-principles (sub-competencies). For example, if the collective principle is "dominating possession in the opponent's half," the sub-principle or sub-competencies would be possession-based exercises related to attacking play, circulation and penetration passing movements, and individual excellence on the ball (to retain possession, exploit space, and dominate in one-on-one situations).

The predicament here becomes how a player or coach can apply the principles of specificity in their own journey within the game. Obviously, this will vary for each person, environment, and circumstance, but the first task is moving from the theoretical to the actual with regards to training. The phrase "train the way you want to play" applies here as the goal is to replicate situations and scenarios in training that will take place in gameplay. Coaches will have to design scenarios and situations that force players to adjust their game to accomplish what is being asked of them in preparation for actual match play.

For example, a small-sided 8v8 game in training has the following game-conditions: one team starts in possession of the ball with the score being 1-0 in their favor. There are five minutes remaining and the playing area is reduced to trigger a series of sub-principles on both sides. For the team in possession, it will push them to manage the clock and retain possession or even push for another goal.

On the other side, the team that is "down by a goal" needs to regain possession and create scoring opportunities to equalize while not conceding another goal. The sub-principles on both teams are all interconnected to the development of all performance dimensions, and achieved through an adopted model of play.

The second task for both players and coaches is to use context as a guide to expose the idiosyncrasies of the actual game against an opponent. In the scenario above, the situations require a specific level of adaptation stemming from the specific exercises to elicit a particular way of playing. An important element regarding development is context. Providing context and allowing the players to figure it out individually and collectively enables them to use their talent and full capacities within a session.

Tendencies and Intensities

Each player has different tendencies and performs at different intensities. In the case of my reaction to negative outcomes, and even the phrase "Don't sweat the small stuff" as a young player, I explored my tendencies as a player and then aimed to affect those tendencies with intensity. I feel intensity is misunderstood and often relegated to being on-par with aggression or being overly-emotional – which (admittedly) I was in my younger years.

However, through developing specific goals that I could devote entire training blocks to addressing, I was able to maintain a high level of concentration to better understand the larger picture. This chapter began with the recollection of a poor individual and collective performance that prompted me to find a way to rehearse specific movements (dribbling at pace, changing directions, executing moves on the ball, etc.) in an alternative environment (a parking lot) that I could transfer back and apply to practice and match play.

In applying this to a more universal context, good coaches take various dimensions of the game into consideration when designing their training exercises. Additionally, good players do the same on an individual level. Both the coach and the player are exhibiting a certain level of deliberate compliance with the principle of specificity in that they understand the purpose of the training as a means towards an understandable and executable objective.

Players can really only experience and adopt the principles and ideas from the coach through specific training-based situations that give them opportunities to perform a given scenario and skill *numerous times*, by reinforcing principles and sub-principles of play.

A key element within a player's performance profile is their tendencies on the pitch. These tendencies reveal almost everything about a player's training experiences, habits, frequencies, and of course, their level of intensity. Players are creatures of habit and will often repeat certain behaviors, decisions, and skills subconsciously. These, too, can reveal much about a player and how they will perform in a given scenario.

Pairing a player's tendencies in the team context is tricky. Personalities, abilities, experience levels, attitudes, and tactical/technical variances from player to player will either align or clash. This is why training should have a "depth" to it that includes systematic repetition of behaviors, decisions, and reactions. In other words, players need a high level of repetition in performing the actions they will execute or be exposed to in a game, in their training.

Oftentimes, players need their tendencies checked and realigned if elements do not fit the playing principles or team model. Repetition can enable players to gain a better understanding of the principles, sub-principles, and overall playing standard within a given team model. A good example is Jurgen Klopp's Borussia Dortmund and Liverpool teams. The team model is one that combines high-pressing (high-energy output) to win the ball, quick interchange and passing patterns in-possession, and the ability to outplay opponents to create numerical advantages in transition.

To prepare for this type of play, the team will likely have repeated the prescribed scenarios to elicit the desired outcomes in training to comply with the team model. Individually, players will have to adjust to the physical and psychological demands so they can successfully replicate the scenarios in training. This is why it's so important to account for the level of intensity with regards to performance expectation.

Scaling intensity is a very important element in high-level development. An individual cannot sustain maximum intensity levels all the time. Additionally, understanding what intensity really is, and how it applies to a player, reveals that intensity is a multi-tiered component. Intensity comes in many forms: the emotional, the physical or physiological, and the mental. As a result, intensity also produces various types of fatigue. Training towards only one or two of the intensity types will leave the other deficient.

Oftentimes, it is difficult to separate each intensity-type fatigue as they are interconnected. However, it is essential for players to understand that almost every physiological intensity will tax their emotional intensity, too. The same is true with mental intensity – or how the player solves problems, anticipates, and makes decisions; when physical fatigue is a factor, the mind will drift, too.

This is where systematic repetition can condition a player to sustain higher levels of intensity fatigue, through repetitive exposure to scenarios and demands that mimic match play. Initiating and sustaining a high level of competitive concentration also taxes the central nervous system. This can yield a positive outcome for players if they can repeat actions with success, which exposes players to a competitive level of pressure in training that gets them close to a competitive reality of a game. As such, Tactical Periodization takes recovery, rest, and competition days into account to offset the intensity of the training scheme.

The scalability of training intensity, while addressing specific intensity types, is perhaps one of the most complex sides of high-level sport.

Introducing different stressors and the role of repetition have to be balanced so as not to burn players out mentally, emotionally, and physically. That being said, training should push them close to the brink in these areas and hold them there briefly to help them advance their resiliency, and increase their ability to navigate through the chaos of tactical and physical fatigue. That process should be repeated so players can recover quickly over the duration of a training block. Sustained assault on the intensities will only lead to performance dips.

Guided Discovery

The last and perhaps most important part of this entire exploration is that of discovery. It is crucial to understand that raw, unguided learning discovery is not a reliable means to develop skill acquisition or learning comprehension. In other words, learning by random chance, luck, or constant failure without any guidance is an exercise of emotional chaos and mental anarchy for anyone, especially young minds.

Guided discovery has been accepted and recognized by learning specialists, top-rated coaches, and pedagogical experts as a superior method of promoting learning in constructivist environments. This entire chapter has really been about guided discovery through the exposure of different principles of specificity, intensity, and tendency models, and a player or coach's ability to apply these towards a team model.

Guided discovery has its challenges such as the type of guidance to provide, the level at which to provide it, along with the frequency of intervention, while still achieving the desired learning outcome and result. Guidance from a coach, teacher, player, or parent is a requirement to help shift the focus and attention onto the target skillset. When performed well, guided discovery provides a framework and structure while allowing for consistency to flourish. With these elements present, the learner can better understand the objectives, and orient themselves to the task of learning within the provided framework.

Top football academies around the world aim not to create robots and drones on the field. They want thinkers and problem solvers – players who can assimilate to a team model while exhibiting a high level of confidence in their creative abilities to the point where they can execute and perform with success. Coaches at these clubs and academies use a tactic called "cluing" to promote players to use their own minds to problem solve and play the game. Frequently, this process is stifled too early when results take precedence over the larger learning goal. When the guided discovery is interrupted, and players cannot reflect and learn, their willingness to think on their own is challenged.

Another method of "cluing" is creating training situations that force players to react and think in a certain way.

This progressive approach allows players to form their own identities on the pitch and does away with over-reliance on the belief that the coach holds all the keys to the game. The coach merely shows players where the doors are located – it is up to the players to find the right keys and walk through themselves. The role of the coach is to create the environment and provide the framework and clues for better learning retention. The team must perform as a unit to think through the game scenarios, but within that unit are individuals who must be given the *freedom* to play within the defined team principles.

The end goal of this entire book is to show how much control a player has on the journey. It is up to each player to aim to improve *their* game and performance by seeking solutions specific to *their* development, not just in the short term but in the future, too. The game holds many lessons for us, and the answers are much more valuable when they are experienced and obtained through guided discovery.

CHAPTER 19: THE FORCE FIELD
OF THE LEARNING CURVE

"Skill acquisition" has become a popular buzz phrase. The term itself can mean different things for different audiences across contexts. Admittedly, this is even more obvious in the digital age, where ideas coalesce daily, and people from all walks of life, experiences, and ability levels can share their thoughts in open and public forums.

On the one hand, such a variety and abundance of viewpoints and information is helpful, and can expedite learning a skill or invite progressive research for people willing to dig into a particular discipline. On the other hand, people tend to get bogged down in both the process and act of acquiring and parsing through materials, plus navigating opinions as to what method is "best" – which leads to people collecting an abundance of information to add to their collections. In my experience, this process leads to paralysis by analysis.

Every worthwhile skill has a learning curve. For some skills, that learning curve is not very steep, and rapid advancement takes place over a short amount of time. For others, that learning curve is steep – and people know this and focus on the difficulty and complexity of it.

I call this the force field of the learning curve. This principle is what separates people from goals.

Henry Ford once said, "Don't expect people to respect you for what you are 'planning' to do."

Growing up, I had a friend named Danny, who wanted to learn how to do a backflip. At recess in elementary school, we saw kids doing audacious dismounts off the swing-set and playground equipment. One day, we saw a boy who was in gymnastics perform a tumbling pass. A tumbling is defined as a sequence or pass that consists of at least two skill elements combined together, such as a round-off to a back handspring into a back-tuck (backflip).

When the boy took off to initiate the tumbling pass, everyone paid attention. Danny, too, was in awe of the athleticism and technique.

Everyone asked the boy how he learned such a skillset. He shrugged and said, "I just practice it at gymnastics."

I thought of the iterations of each movement and realized it was probably too complex to learn myself. Danny, on the other hand, had a different mentality. Danny had what we have identified as a growth mindset, and while I did not (and still don't) possess a fixed mindset, Danny decided to learn how to tumble with no hesitation.

In life, as in sport, there is a point at which people will either be repelled by the force field of the learning curve, or they will find a way to enter a zone of total commitment. That day, after school, Danny and I walked home, and we stopped at a nearby playground. Danny stepped up on a small park bench and attempted a backflip. He landed on his back and laid sprawled out on the tanbark. He got up and tried again and again. Each time he attempted to do a backflip, he landed with an awkwardly painful thud.

But, he remained undeterred and his determination pushed him to make further attempts. Finally, after an hour of watching Danny try and fail, I told him I was going home. Danny stayed at the park. The following day at school, during recess, Danny walked off to a corner and started attempting backflips off of benches. In less than 24 hours, he had gone from general intrigue and not knowing how to perform a complex movement to executing it off apparatus with confidence.

The point of this story is important as it relates to the practices, principles, theories, and stories in this book. Most people got caught up in the thought about how one could learn to tumble. The first step would be to sign-up for a tumbling or gymnastic class, followed by some rudimentary lessons by a trained teacher or coach on a soft surface with spotters. This would take place over several days or weeks to gain proficiency.

Danny, on the other hand, bypassed that entire thought process. He saw what we wanted to learn, and he literally found a launching pad for his journey to attain a new skill. The factors that others would need as requirements or inputs – such as a coach, soft mats, technical training, and formalized settings – were not factors for Danny. In fact, his approach forced him to commit to the process wholeheartedly. When you're launching yourself off a park bench, over hard ground with no formal training, your focus has to be all-in on the micro-processes of the movement.

Over the years, I've seen how these suppositional force fields separate people from a terrain that cannot be reached by taking shortcuts. You can't buy your way into learning a backflip in a day. Just like one cannot fake their way into becoming a better player. You have to train and focus and commit to it. In his mind, Danny knew he couldn't fake his way to executing a backflip.

The Problem with Planning

If you take nothing else from this book, or at least this chapter, know that over-planning leads to stagnation when it comes to learning how to become a better player. People tend to believe reading a book about swimming will make them a better swimmer. That is called "Dry Swimming," and while it helps one learn about swimming, it does not make them a better swimmer. For that, they must get in the water and start moving. They may fail and struggle – these are certainties – but buying more swimming books, reading about swimming online, buying new goggles and swimming equipment, joining a fancy gym (while marginally important) will not make someone a better swimmer. You have to get in the water and swim.

Too many players dedicate themselves to "Dry Swimming." The whole point of this book is to open up the avenues for finding ways to play the game through intense persistence, focus, repetition, game-realistic scenarios, and – above all else – through creative, sustainable, and enjoyable means. For most of our lives, we are taught to think that the more time we spend preparing to play, the better we will be once the whistle blows. This makes sense in theory, but there is one major fallacy to the notion.

Over-planning does not lead to action.

Players often get bogged down with overthinking about the skills they want or need to learn. Their parents recruit different resources and pay for applications on their smartphones, but at the end of the day, the success of the game can be distilled down to a player's ability and relationship with the ball.

When I first set out to write about my experience getting thousands of touches a day on the ball, in various game-realistic scenarios and settings, people challenged the validity of the method. Most were stuck in the planning stage. Others spent more time trying to debunk the methods, having never attempted any of the principles or applicable training scenarios to their own approaches. They tried to architect every nuance and movement into a rigid model. The game, however, is fluid and unpredictable. There is no clear-cut path for any player to take to reach the top levels of their respective ability or potential. For a player to improve their ability on the ball, they need to have a ball at their feet. After that, they must immerse themselves in the process.

Going back to the story about my friend Danny, consider how many players will only train if there is a coach, a pristine field, beautiful weather, and a playbook or script to joystick their every movement and action. That would comprise much of the modern youth game in many countries. While these inputs are important for learning, they will not always be available.

The force field of the learning curve is often unrecognizable, too. Players have no idea they are the ones holding themselves back and impeding progress. Over-planning makes a person rather inflexible and stifles creativity. The more you require the game to be planned out for you, the more you subscribe to a life of inflexibility. You become too attached to "the plan" and when the plan forces you to adjust or deviate, it deters progress.

Soccer is a game that never plays out as planned. In this sense, it is much like life. Over the countless stories I've shared about my time playing and coaching the game, the one aspect that I believe to be most important is being steadfast about your goals while being flexible in your methods.

Elite Mentality

The force field of the learning curve, as explained with regards to learning a specific skill, is only part of the process. How do we apply it to soccer or, more specifically, meaningful competition? After all, training and preparation are stepping stones to match play. For this, I decided to seek out someone that understands this more than most.

One of my former collegiate teammates who captained the team when I first showed up is a man named Adam Jones. Adam had a stellar collegiate career and went on to play professionally before making his transition to the corporate world. As a high-level player with professional playing experience and as someone who still trains with a similar consistency and intensity for endurance and strength-based pursuits to this day – long after hanging up his boots – I knew his experience could prove helpful.

We talked about the article that kicked this whole project off (the one on immersive and systematic repetition-based technical training). Adam was interested in the parallels between soccer and other disciplines, too, and we also discussed and evaluated the criticisms that have followed me and my work since 2014, which remain valuable examples of the importance of exploring an idea in-depth.

"The article that you wrote many years ago… you're only really having to edit a little bit here and there to show how timeless true principles are," explained Adam. "Truth always stands the test of time. And the fact that the time has passed and the principles are still intact -- there's something to be said about that."

Much like Danny, who took a direct route to de-complicate his development towards a specific skill, Adam recalled the training philosophy of his club team towards developing match fitness. There are many ways to achieve high fitness levels, but match fitness is different from other types of fitness. The game is full of nuances and cues that are difficult, if not impossible, to train unless a match is played or simulated. To prepare for a grueling schedule in the heat of the American Southwest and Texas, Adam's club team (which was considered one of the elite clubs not only in Texas but nationally) focused on a progressive model of training. It started with dynamic technical work before playing actual matches as often as possible in training.

Because his team routinely played against top sides from around the country, including one of the most talented US U-17 national team squads – many of whom were part of the 1999 class that had future pros and senior national team standouts like Landon Donovan, DaMarcus Beasley, Oguchi Onyewu, Bobby Convey, and Kyle Beckerman – the philosophy and playing level required players to be used to training for the exact thing that mattered most – match play.

"One of the best club teams I played on had one major philosophy, and it was Match Fitness. Many times a week we'd get to a session and do a dynamic warm-up, 20-to-30 minutes of high-intensity technical sessions in small groups; lots of movement, three-to-five people in a group. Then from there, a 90-100 minute match. The coach would generally pit us against his other team that was one year younger in a 90-minute match – high intensity."

At high levels of play, much of what is trained can detract from the overall objective, which is to play meaningful competition. This is why every time I have mentioned technical or physical training in this book, I have always made it clear that it has to be game-realistic and applicable.

Adam's experience echoes these points.

"We didn't run sprints for fitness, we didn't run 10-mile runs, we didn't do suicide sprints. We played as many 90-minute matches as possible because that's what all other fitness would try to simulate. Now, I'm sure a lot of our competition pulled sleds, did plyometrics, all sorts of different drills that I've done on other teams. But achieving superior match fitness put us above almost everyone we played in 90 minutes because we were simulating it often. When you can train towards the very thing you need to do – and do it well – others have difficulty matching that level and competing for 90-minutes."

Adam also addressed the conundrum that players don't have enough time to train at the levels or in the manners discussed in this book. As I've found, much of the criticism comes from those who have not experienced the levels of the game beyond a certain point. Of course, my own experience has its ceiling, which is why Adam's opinion is important as he reached much higher levels as a player.

"Parents who say that their children don't have time are parents who probably were not high achievers in anything growing up. They were probably middle-of-the-road, playing the clarinet in marching band, cross-country, soccer, wrestling, basketball – it doesn't matter. If they were a high achiever at any one of those, and they did any one of those at elite levels, they would know that there is never enough time. If you are not obsessively training all the time, working at the craft all the time, then you will not achieve anything significant or phenomenal."

Much like others who have grown up in high-level playing environments and reached the professional level, Adam shed light on what the truly elite level (and required mentality) is like, which is valuable for those who haven't reached that level.

"When you get to an elite level of anything, you realize that everyone is so good and has the will to win, you're going to have to turn on every switch, take advantage of every pocket of time, so then maybe, you'll get lucky and beat them when it matters most. The players that I played with who were great, they never quarreled over "how much time is it going to take?"

"They were always concerned that they were never doing enough. They *needed* more reps, they *needed* more ball work; their mindset told them, "just five more sprints, just give me five more I need to make sure that I'm ready." At that level, they're so devastated by losses, they're so compelled by their ambitious vision to be a champion, that they're not worried about *anything* except that they might not be doing enough."

This book is based upon the principle of "What gets measured gets managed" and training towards a specific skill or task extends well beyond the field.

"In any operational corporate environment, what gets measured gets done. People are excellent at wasting time," Adam said.

"Mobile devices, commercials, bathroom breaks – if you really started measuring everything and how much time everything took, and it really came to be like a world-ending scenario where you had to spend every waking minute doing something – you would realize how much time you had. If your child's life was on the line and you had to run for 48 hours or they would die, you would find a way to run 48 hours. It's all about that urgency and desperation. Time is lost everywhere and unless you're disciplined and measuring things – and if you're not really pushing people to do more than they think they can do – you're going to get average out of people, at best."

It's Just a Ball

I often think about that night in San Francisco, when I was at one of my lowest moments, where I found my love for the game again. Running through the misty and drizzled cityscape with a ball at my feet removed all complexity from the game. For many of us, there exists a relationship between who we are and what we do with our time. In the words of Heraclitus, "Day by day, what you do is who you become."

Most people will play the game for a set period of time before we move on to other aspects of life. Some of us are blessed and cursed with an obsession with the game within the game. Our best moments are likely lost in the sands of time, uncaptured on any highlight reels, devoid of any tangible record. For us, we must keep that image and memory alive through our celebration of the world's game by whatever means suit us.

In closing, just remember that the game is what you make it. There are lessons to be learned from challenging yourself, and soccer offers us an ever-evolving landscape to learn about who we are as people. When I first set out to write this book, it was never about "how to become a pro" or *the secret* to unlocking your potential. This book is not a how-to guide, it's an exploration of thought, experience, and storytelling.

This book will always be about the Everyman in the game. You are the Everyman character in your own story. As the protagonist, you will go through life as a humble individual while facing an extraordinary set of challenges. You have the potential to be exceptional, but as the Everyman archetype, you will have to mount an exceptional response to each challenge before you, as it relates to not only the game but to life.

Never forget that even when you acquire special abilities that help you, it's important to find a way to love what you do. There is an art to taking action. By discovering what action to take, you can home in on your purpose. For some, it will literally be to become the best player they can be. For most of us, however, it will be about finding out more about ourselves (and life) by using the ball as a vehicle of self-discovery.

Some of our other 25+ books for soccer coaches

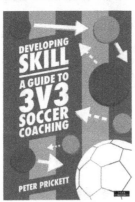

BUILDING A SUCCESSFUL
HIGH
SCHOOL
SPORTS PROGRAM

DeAngelo Wiser

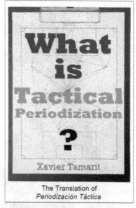

What
is
Tactical
Periodization
?

Xavier Tamarit

The Translation of
Periodización Táctica

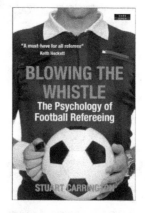

"A must-have for all referees"
Keith Hackett

BLOWING THE
WHISTLE
The Psychology of
Football Refereeing

STUART CARRINGTON

Vasilis Papadakis

Pre-Season
Soccer
Training

A Seven Week,
50 Session
Guide to
Building For The
New Season

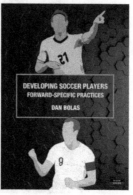

DEVELOPING SOCCER PLAYERS
FORWARD-SPECIFIC PRACTICES
DAN BOLAS

Scientific Approaches to
Goalkeeping in Football
Age-Specific Goalkeeper Development

Andy
Elleray

Foundation Phase	7-11
Youth Development Phase	12-16
Professional Development Phase	17-21

WINNING YOUR
PLAYERS
THROUGH TRUST,
LOYALTY, AND
RESPECT

DeAngelo Wiser

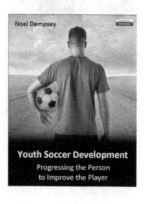

Noel Dempsey

Youth Soccer Development
Progressing the Person
to Improve the Player

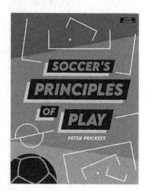

SOCCER'S
PRINCIPLES
OF PLAY
PETER PRICKETT